# Eternal *life*

Can you really be certain you have it?

R. LARRY MOYER

*This book is dedicated to all those who want to know beyond the shadow of any doubt that their eternity will be spent in the presence of the King of Kings.*

# TABLE OF CONTENTS

# Biblical Distinctions

# Concluding Thoughts

# INTRODUCTION

# INTRODUCTION

Many people experience the hardest and worst struggle they have ever had. They struggle with knowing for certain that they are going to heaven. When that struggle is at its worst, there are those who have been so frank as to call it "hell on earth."

Some want to be certain that they are what the Bible calls "saved" but are uncertain how to be sure. They have heard all kinds of "gospels" and are confused which is the right one.

Others would claim to be believers, but they are uncertain if they are genuinely saved. One day they are convinced that they will live forever with Jesus Christ; the next day they are not as sure. They pass a fatal car accident and wonder, "Where would I be if something happened to me?" Even though they have gone through motions such as repeating the "sinner's prayer" or responding to an altar call at a church, doubt still lingers. The pendulum in their mind consistently swings from "He loves me" to "He loves me not."

Numerous times people have sat in front of me with tears running down their cheeks as they told me of their uncertainty about their salvation. For some it has been a lifelong struggle.

My dear wife, Tammy, was one of those — and here she was marrying an evangelist! So why would I marry someone who was not certain of her salvation? If she were not a believer, how could I marry her when the Bible explicitly says, "Do not be unequally yoked together with unbelievers"? (2 Corinthians 6:14)

Because by that time, having already counseled many individuals about their salvation, I knew why and where she was struggling. I simply needed to help her think biblically and I knew her doubts would be behind her. Quite honestly, it did not take long. A brief time into our marriage she became as certain of heaven as though she were already there. Now, she *never* has a question about where she will be when she dies. And being certain of her salvation has increased her desire to tell others how they can be certain of theirs.

This book is written for those who want to put the question of where they will spend their eternity forever behind them and look forward to seeing Jesus Christ face to face. You may be one who has never settled the issue but want to. Or you may be one who "thinks" you have settled the issue but are not sure.

Once you understand why biblically your salvation is guaranteed, you can shout and sing with millions of others, "Blessed assurance, Jesus is mine." It may cause you also to reach out to others with the Good News. With your salvation settled in your mind, you want their salvation to be settled in theirs.

# CHAPTER ONE

## *So why are so many uncertain?*

Before we discuss how and why one can be as certain of heaven as though they are already there, it helps to ask, "But why are so many people uncertain?"

## There are a number of reasons.

### 1

Some have not fully grasped the message of the gospel and what the Bible means by "believe." Unless those two are understood, one will never have the assurance of his salvation that God wants him to have. If he does not understand anything else in the Scriptures, to be certain of salvation he must understand the most important message of the Bible that is referred to as the "Good News" and then the response God desires from us when He uses the word "believe." Along with that, we must examine the confusion that surrounds the word "repentance." A clear understanding of the biblical truths surrounding these subjects enables one to clearly understand what one must do to be saved.

## 2

Too often even after responding to Christ's call to salvation, we look at ourselves and the promises we have made to God in order to feel certain of our salvation. We think of the temptations we promised to say "no" to, the ways we were determined to "clean up our act," and the new habits we wanted to form. Failure in any of those areas then takes away the assurance of our salvation. Satan, our enemy, delights in having us think in that direction.

Instead, we must do what the Scriptures do — look at the basis for our eternal security as it is found in the deity of Christ and the promises God has made to us. The more one understands how these two make us eternally secure in Christ, the more excited one can be that we are forever His. Assurance of salvation is found as we look to Him and His promises to us, not to ourselves and our promises to Him.

## 3

Others have been the victims of wrong teaching. Ideas have been shared as though they are biblical when, in fact, they are not. Some thoughts or ideas have been handed down from one generation to another and are tradition-based rather than based on God's Word. These must be carefully examined so we know that we are directed by Scripture, not tradition.

4

Still others have suffered from a misunderstanding of particular paragraphs of Scripture. We must look at these Scriptures in context. What God is actually saying versus what a person understood Him to say may be two different things.

5

Some doubt that they are saved because they do not always "feel saved." They must understand that salvation is based on fact, not feeling.

6

Another reason is the failure to grasp two important biblical distinctions — the distinction between entering the Christian life and living the Christian life. There is a difference between salvation and discipleship. While they have a relationship to one another, they are also distinctive concepts. The more one is clear on these distinctions the more assured he will be of his salvation. He will also find himself more motivated to live a life committed to following Christ.

No book on the certainty of our salvation would be complete without addressing the issue that if our salvation is guaranteed, why "sell out" for Christ. What more is there? The more we grasp the answer to that question the more excited we can be

**What God is actually saying versus what a person understood Him to say may be two different things.**

with building on the security we have in Christ. We can then be equally excited about becoming every inch the person God wants us to be as we await that time when we will see Him face to face.

So, let's examine each of these topics. A person who understood these issues from a biblical perspective was once asked, "When you see the Lord, what do you think is the first thing He will ask you?" The man answered, "Oh, I don't think He will ask a thing. I think He will simply look at me and say, 'He's mine!'"

The more we understand our eternal security and have the assurance of it upon trusting Christ, the more we can look forward with excitement to a day when we will see Him face to face knowing that, even now, He is rejoicing in the fact, "You're mine."

●  ●  ●

## QUESTIONS FOR REFLECTION

1. When you think of times you have struggled with your salvation, which of the reasons given would be most appropriate to your situation?

2. When you think of others who have struggled with their salvation, which of the reasons given might be most appropriate to their situation?

# CHAPTER TWO

## *An important clarification*

As we get started, we need to make an important clarification.

The words "eternal security" and "assurance" are often used interchangeably. It is easy to understand why, yet this can be confusing. For example, some say, "I just do not understand how you can be certain that once you have come to Christ, that you will never lose your salvation. 'Once saved always saved' just sounds too good to be true."

Then others say, "I believe in eternal security, I just do not have assurance of *my* salvation." What they are saying is, "I believe that if I am genuinely saved, I am His forever. He will never disown me. I just don't know for sure if I am saved."

So, by "eternal security" they are referring to the biblical teaching that to be His is to be His forever. We cannot lose our salvation. By the term "assurance" they are referring to their personal confidence that they have done what they needed to do to be saved — that they were sincere, that they fully understood the plan of salvation, that there is enough evidence in their life that they are saved, and a host of other items.

What many fail to realize is how eternal security and assurance of our salvation are interconnected. The reason many lack assurance is because they have failed to grasp the security we have in Christ.

**What many fail to realize is how eternal security and assurance of our salvation are interconnected.**

The more one understands the basis of eternal security as it relates to the message and our response to it, the teaching of Scripture regarding salvation, and the need of handling Scripture in proper context, the more assurance one has. What God is actually saying versus what a person understood Him to say may be two different things.

As will be explained, the Bible does not disconnect the two.

The more we understand the Scriptural teaching in regard to our eternal salvation, we realize that there is one thing we need never doubt. That is that as long as we have received God's gracious and generous offer, we are eternally His. There are some things in life about which we cannot be absolutely certain. Our relationship with Him need not be one of those.

One thing might be added. Some people doubt their salvation because they doubt everything. They doubt that their mate loves them, they doubt that their children respect them, they doubt if their employer is going to keep them, they doubt if they have the ability others think they do. *They don't merely doubt their salvation; they doubt anything and everything.* This book may not help such a person because the problem is much deeper than the scope of this book. But I would remind such a person that he may have reason to doubt anything anyone says. But there is no reason to doubt what God says. God speaks with a tongue that never slips and makes promises that never fail.

## *Conclusion*

Simply put, the more we understand the "why" of our eternal security and the promises of God connected with it, the more thrilled we can be. We are assured of our salvation because He has assured us, "You are mine — forever!" Eternal security and assurance — two ideas that support one another.

**Eternal security and assurance — two ideas that support one another.**

●  ●  ●

## QUESTIONS FOR REFLECTION

1. How would you explain the distinction between eternal security and assurance of one's salvation?

2. How should the interconnection of eternal security and assurance personally impact every believer?

# CHAPTER THREE

## Why is the assurance of our salvation so essential?

There are many areas of life where uncertainty is not a major issue. But the matter of our eternal salvation and our assurance of it is not one of those. No issue needs more certainty than that of where one's eternal destiny will be spent — with God or forever apart from God.

Numerous reasons for that could be given. But the main reason can be reduced to one sentence. *No one is promised tomorrow.* In fact, it would be better to say that there is not one person on earth who is promised the *next moment.* Nearly everyone who passes from this life into the next thought they had at least another year, month, week, day, or moment to live. That is why where we are going when we die cannot be something that we have an *ounce* of insecurity about.

The business people of James' day loved to brag about where they were going, when they would leave, how long they would be there, what they would do, and how much they would profit financially. James gave them a stern warning, "Come now, you who say, 'Today or tomorrow we will go to such and such a city,

**In fact, it would be better to say that there is not one person on earth who is promised *the next moment.***

spend a year there, buy and sell, and make a profit'; whereas you do not know what will happen tomorrow. For what is your life? It is even a vapor that appears for a little time and then vanishes away. Instead you ought to say, 'If the Lord wills, we shall live and do this or that.'" (James 4:13-15) Life can end so suddenly.

On top of that, time here on earth is rather short — 60, 70, 80, maybe 100 years. Time on the other side of the grave is awfully long. It's called eternity. We would be foolish to not be certain where that eternity will be spent, particularly when there is no second chance. As Hebrews 9:27 tells us, "And as it is appointed for men to die once, but after this the judgment." Life forever will either be spent in the presence of God or separated from Him.

**The issue of where we will spend our eternity dare not be a guessing game or something one is simply optimistic about.**

Absolute knowledge of where that eternity will be spent is necessary *now*. The issue of where we will spend our eternity dare not be a guessing game or something one is simply optimistic about. It is the *one* issue that should never be dismissed to be dealt with at a later time.

## *Conclusion*

We do not know when our lives will end and our eternity with or away from God will begin. Life is uncertain. So, the assurance we have of our salvation is second to no other matter. We must know where we are going when we die and know that *now*!

• • •

## QUESTIONS FOR REFLECTION

1.  In one sentence, why is the assurance of your salvation so essential?

2.  How does the warning given in James 4:13-15 impact the need for assurance of your salvation?

# THE FOUNDATION
## OF OUR SALVATION

# Chapter Four

## *What is the Good News?*

Many are unaware that the guarantee of our salvation is found in the heart of the message that brings people to Christ — the gospel — the Good News. Let's look first at what the gospel is and then how it is foundational to our assurance of salvation.

The Bible is not simply the gospel. The Bible is a whole lot more than the gospel — how to raise your family, how to honor God with your money, how to love your neighbor or your enemy (sometimes the same people!), end-time events, church policy and government, creation and historical events, and paragraphs related to joy, sorrow, trials, hardships, patience, prayer, life inside and outside the family of God. The list of subjects the Bible covers is extremely long. After all, the Bible is a total of 66 books.

The Bible is not the gospel; instead, the Bible *contains* the gospel. The gospel can be defined in ten words as seen from 1 Corinthians 15: 3-5. There we are told, "For I delivered to you first of all that which I also received: that Christ died for our sins according to the Scriptures, and that He was buried, and that He rose again the third day according to the Scriptures, and that He was seen by Cephas, then by the twelve." Note that there are four verbs that surround the gospel.

Christ **died** for our sins. "For" there means "instead of" or "on behalf of." He died in our place. Had He not died, we would have.

He was our substitute. They crucified Him where they should have crucified us. The nails that should have been driven through our hands and feet were driven through His. "According to the Scriptures" means His death was a fulfillment of what the prophet Isaiah predicted 700 years earlier. Isaiah 53:5-6 foretold, "But He was wounded for our transgressions, He was bruised for our iniquities; the chastisement for our peace was upon Him, and by His stripes we are healed. All we like sheep have gone astray; we have turned, every one, to his own way; and the Lord has laid on Him the iniquity of us all."

He was **buried.** That is the proof that He died. There were those who witnessed that burial.

He **rose** again the third day. The word "rose" contains the idea that He rose and is still risen. There will never be a newspaper produced in Jerusalem that says the body of Christ has just been discovered. "According to the Scriptures" is again a fulfillment of what the Old Testament prophesied. Psalm 16:10 tells us, "For You will not leave my soul in Sheol, nor will you allow Your Holy One to see corruption." God was not surprised by the crucifixion, and neither was He surprised by the resurrection.

He was **seen.** As His burial is proof that He died, the fact that He was seen is proof that He arose. The greatest testimony one can have in court is an eyewitness. The Scriptures welcome us into the courtroom and give a list of those who saw Him. These were not ones who merely heard about the risen Christ, these were ones that *saw* the risen Christ.

So, the gospel can be contained in ten words. **Christ died for our sins and rose from the dead.** His burial is proof that He died and the fact that He was seen is proof that He arose. But whereas the Bible is 66 books, the gospel is ten words — *Christ died for our sins and rose from the dead.*

*So how does that impact our security and assurance?*

The ramifications of that are fourfold.

First, it was not just anybody dying on the cross. That would not have accomplished anything. One sinner cannot pay for the sins of another. We all have sins of our own for which we have to pay. Instead, it had to be somebody completely without sin who could take the place of somebody who had sinned.

The only one who met that requirement of being absolutely perfect was Jesus Christ, the Son of God. God's perfect Son died in our place. That is what atoned for our sins. John the Baptist declared upon seeing Him, "Behold! The Lamb of God who takes away the sin of the world!" (John 1:29) Although it was a difficult death for Him to die on a cross, He died willingly in our place. He Himself declared, "Therefore My Father loves Me, because I lay down My life that I may take it again. No one takes it from Me, but I lay it down of Myself. I have power to lay it down, and

> **But whereas the Bible is 66 books, the gospel is ten words — *Christ died for our sins and rose from the dead.***

I have power to take it again. This command I have received from my Father." (John 10:17-18)

*Hence our salvation and the assurance of it has absolutely nothing to do with what we have done for Him. It has everything to do with what He as our perfect substitute has done for us.*

Secondly, our security and assurance are based on something that has happened — not something that might happen. It is based on historical fact, not theory. The resurrection is one of the most, if not *the* most, attested facts of history. Dr. Haddon Robinson in a "Focal Point" paper for the Christian Medical Society along with others quoted Thomas Arnold (longtime headmaster of Rugby School, the author of a three-volume history of Rome, and appointed to the Chair of Modern History at Oxford University) as saying, "I have been used for many years to study the histories of other times, and to examine and weigh the evidence of those who have written about them, and I know of no one fact in the history of mankind which is proved by better and fuller evidence of every sort, to the understanding of a fair inquirer than the fact that Christ died and rose again from the dead." Having risen from the grave Himself, Christ had every right to declare, "Because I live, you will live also." (John 14:19)

*So, our salvation is based on a proven, objective fact, not subjective experience, on what is past and done, not what is future and undone.*

Thirdly, when Christ died on the cross as our substitute, He announced, "It is finished." (John 19:30) The Greek word translated "finished" is *tetelestai*. It means paid in full. Those who paid their taxes in New Testament times were given a receipt with the word *tetelestai* stamped on it. There was nothing left to pay. The debt had been paid in full. Likewise with our sin, there is nothing left to pay. We have to simply accept His payment.

**On the cross, Christ did not make the down payment; He made the full payment.**

On the cross, Christ did not make the down payment; He made the full payment. There is nothing we can do to add to what He has already done. The wrath of God against our sin was forever met. That is why He arose the third day — to prove that God was satisfied with His Son's sin payment for our sin problem.

*God was completely satisfied with what His son did in our place. Nothing you have done, can do, will do, or promise to do can pay for what is already paid.*

Finally, He died for all — no exceptions! 1 John 2:2 tells us, "And He Himself is the propitiation for our sins, and not for ours only but also for the whole world." 2 Corinthians 5:15 begins, "And He died for all..." No sinner is excluded regardless of his or her background, behavior, skin color, language, or nationality. His love is unconditional. He was the substitute for anybody anywhere, everybody everywhere.

That itself figures into our eternal security and assurance of it. He loves us regardless of who we are and what we have done. Once He saves us, He would not toss us back on the basis of how we perform. That would be everything but unconditional love.

I spoke with a father who did not believe in the eternal security of the believer. I asked him a simple question, "What would one of your three daughters have to do for you not to love them anymore?" He answered, "Nothing! I will always love them regardless of what they do." I then said, "But suppose one of them denies that you are her dad? Would that no longer make her your daughter?" He answered, "No way. She would still be my daughter." I then explained, "What you have just told me is that you know more about love than God does. You would not disown her based on her behavior but yet you are convinced Christ would reject us if we do not perform properly as His children or got so far out of fellowship because of a bitter life experience that we even denied that we knew Him." He saw the fallacy of his thinking and took God at His Word — to be His was to be His forever.

*The security we have in Christ is tied into the unconditional love of the One who died for us. Unconditional love never stops being unconditional. He loves us unconditionally before we are saved, and He loves us unconditionally after we are saved.*

*What does all this mean?*

**We are accepted by God based on His Son's perfection — a fact that cannot be altered by our imperfection.**

We are accepted by God not based on our performance but based on His. It has nothing to do with us; it has everything to do with Him and His unconditional love. In accepting us, God does not look ahead to see how we are going to do; He looks back on what His Son had already done. We are not saved on the basis of our performance, but on the basis of His. Neither our good performance nor our poor performance once we have come to Christ can change anything. We are accepted by God based on His Son's perfection — a fact that cannot be altered by our imperfection.

Hence the assurance we can have that once we have come to Him we are His, is so intricately wrapped up in the message itself. That message has nothing to do with us; it has everything to do with Him. *Christ died for our sins and rose from the dead.* I owed a debt I could not pay. He paid in full a debt He did not owe.

When we lack assurance, it is often because our focus has gone to the wrong place — what is future, undone, and uncertain, instead of what is past, done, and certain.

## Conclusion

When thinking about our salvation, all thoughts need to go to Him and what He has done, not ourselves and what we have done or plan to do. Our salvation is based on something past, final, documented, and complete. It cannot be emphasized enough that the security of our salvation and our assurance that we are His has nothing to do with us; it has everything to do with Him. It is based on objective truth, not subjective experience.

● ● ●

## Questions for Reflection

1.  What are the ten words that define the gospel?

2.  How does the death of His Son being an objective fact in the past impact the assurance of our salvation in the present?

3.  How does the death of God's Son on a cross demonstrate the unconditional love of God? What bearing should that have on our life now?

4.  How does Christ's performance on the cross versus our performance impact the assurance of our salvation?

5.  Where should our mind and thoughts go if at any time we struggle with our salvation?

# CHAPTER FIVE

## *What does the Bible mean by "believe"?*

Not only is an understanding of the gospel foundational to our security and assurance, so is an understanding of what the Bible means by "believe" — a subject often referred to as saving faith. Because many are confused by what the word "believe" means, they are uncertain that they have done the right thing in appropriating His free gift of eternal life.

The one book of the Bible written specifically to explain how we obtain eternal life is the Gospel of John. We know that was John's purpose because we are told, "But these are written that you may believe that Jesus is the Christ, the Son of God, and that believing you may have life in His name." (John 20:31) John uses the word "believe" 98 times in this book, sometimes up to three times in one verse, such as in John 3:18. "He who believes in Him is not condemned; but he who does not believe is condemned already, because he has not believed in the name of the only begotten Son of God."

The Greek word used for believe throughout John is *pisteuo*. It comes from the Greek word *pistis* which means faith. It means to so consider something to be true that it is worthy of one's trust.

In contrast to what the biblical word "believe" means, the modern day use of the word can mean nothing more than a possibility.

A person says, "I believe it is going to rain today." She means, "I think there is a strong possibility that it is going to rain."

That "possibility" idea is not what the Bible means by "believe." "Believe", in the Bible, is based on the truth of His death and resurrection. That is why the word that best communicates what the Bible means by believe is the word "trust." We come to God as sinners, understand that Jesus Christ died in our place for our sins and arose the third day, accept that as being true, and *trust in Him alone* to save us. Our heart attitude is "If He cannot take me to heaven, I am going to hell. He is all I have. I believe that He and He alone is my *only* hope of eternal life." We are convinced of the truth of Acts 4:12, "Nor is there salvation in any other, for there is no other name under heaven given among men by which we must be saved."

**Hence the idea behind the word "believe" as it is used in an evangelistic context is *"be satisfied with the thing that satisfies God."***

Hence the idea behind the word "believe" as it is used in an evangelistic context is *"be satisfied with the thing that satisfies God."* 1 John 2:2 explains, "And He Himself is the propitiation for our sins, and not for ours only but also for the whole world." Propitiation means satisfaction. God was satisfied with what His Son did on a cross when our sins were "paid in full." God is now asking us to believe — to be satisfied with the thing that satisfied God.

The moment we transfer our trust from whatever it was on as our means of eternal life (such as the good works we have done, the church attendance we have had, the baptism we experienced, or the sacraments we have taken) and place our trust in Christ to save us, we have appropriated His free gift of eternal life. We have done what the Bible calls "believed." We have agreed with God about who His Son is and what He did on our behalf when He died as our substitute. *We are satisfied with the thing that satisfies God.*

That is why if one *accepts it as true* who Christ is and what He did on our behalf, *wants* to be saved, and *knows how* to be saved, it is impossible not to be saved. Such a person is indeed satisfied with the thing that satisfies God. He has trusted Christ. We dare not make it more difficult than it is.

*It's not Christ plus, but Christ period.*

Being satisfied with the thing that satisfies God means our trust is in Christ *alone* to save us. Not Christ plus our church attendance, Christ plus our baptism, Christ plus our good life, or Christ plus the sacraments we have taken. We are saved through Christ *period*, not through Christ *plus*. On the cross He did not make the down payment for our sin; He made the full payment. God was not satisfied with what His Son did along with what we do. He was satisfied with His Son's death and that *alone* as sufficient payment for our sins.

To trust in something else *in addition* to Christ means that we are not satisfied with the thing that satisfied God. We have not believed and therefore are not His. He was only satisfied with one thing — His Son's death on our behalf. *That and that alone is what paid for our sins.* As Hebrews 10:12-14 states, "But this Man, after He had offered one sacrifice for sins forever, sat down at the right hand of God, from that time waiting till His enemies are made His footstool. For by one offering He has perfected forever those who are being sanctified."

That is why we are told in Ephesians 2:8-9, "For by grace you have been saved through faith, and that not of yourselves; it is the gift of God, not of works, lest anyone should boast." If the smallest amount of anything we are or do was part of what got us to heaven, we could brag, "God did His part, and I did mine." But since salvation is *solely* the result of Christ's work on the cross on our behalf, all the bragging rights go to God, and He alone gets the glory.

If eternal life were based on anything other than Christ alone, it also would not be grace. No verse in the Bible says that any clearer than Romans 11:6. "And if by grace, then it is no longer of works; otherwise grace is no longer grace. But if it is of works, it is no longer grace; otherwise, work is no longer work." Nor would it be a gift. Instead, eternal life would be a trade-off. God is not making a bargain or offering a trade-off; instead He is extending a gift through His grace.

Furthermore, if our eternal life was based on anything other than Christ alone, we could never know we are going to heaven. He did His part but what if we do not do ours or just thought we did our part?

*Analytical people sometimes struggle the most.*

I have found that analytical people who are extremely introspective sometimes struggle the most with their salvation. Their strength becomes a weakness. The reason is that they analyze and inspect everything — to death! They say to themselves, "Did I believe enough? Was I sincere enough? How do I know that I am actually trusting Him to save me?"

I often advise them to look at their salvation from a different perspective. I encourage them to ask themselves, "Do I think my good works will get me into heaven? Do I believe that a person is saved through being baptized? Do I believe that my church attendance will get me to heaven? Do I believe that I need something *in addition* to Christ to be saved?" If the answer to those is a resounding "no" and they understand that He alone saves, they are satisfied with the thing that satisfies God.

*You do not have to know the date.*

A person may not know when that moment was that he or she crossed the line of faith. Nowhere does the Bible say that if one does not know the date they were saved, they are not saved. There *was* a specific second that you crossed the line of faith and when you see the Savior face to face,

**Nowhere does the Bible say that if one does not know the date they were saved, they are not saved.**

He will be able to tell you when that was. But if you are satisfied with the thing that satisfied God, you are saved regardless of when you crossed the line. The reason is that your trust is in Christ alone to save you.

I sincerely believe that there are many people who did not cross the line of faith when they thought they did. The moment when they actually understood that His death on the cross was sufficient payment for everything wrong they have done or will do may have been days, weeks, months, or even years later — or earlier. But regardless of when and where it happened, their trust is in Christ alone to save them, and they are forever His.

Again, there is a specific second that we cross from death into life. But nowhere does Scripture say that you have to know when that moment was. Assurance comes from trusting a Person, not knowing the point of time when that occurred.

*The circumstances or setting is not the issue.*

Understanding what the Bible means by "believe" clarifies in one's mind why one is not saved by saying the sinner's prayer, walking forward in a church, or signing a card at an evangelistic outreach.

First of all, there is no "sinner's prayer" in the Bible. Prayer may be a means by which we verbalize to God that we are trusting Christ to save us, but we are saved by trusting Christ not by saying a certain prayer. A prayer is not what satisfied God. A person who did not understand that, and felt that saying a certain prayer (called "the sinner's prayer" in some circles) is what saved, asked me, "Will God honor the prayer if the grammar is not right?" He had so many doubts about his salvation because his trust was not in Christ but instead in the prayer that he prayed. I explained the salvation message to him, he trusted Christ, and is now in full-time ministry.

Even when I have the privilege of leading someone to Christ, I encourage them to pray with me as they tell God that they are trusting Christ alone to save them. I have found that verbalizing it in prayer cements in his or her own mind what they have done. But before we pray, I always remind them that saying a prayer does not save anyone. We are saved the second we trust Christ alone as our only way to heaven. At that point we are satisfied with what satisfies God. For that reason, I am convinced that most people are saved before they ever pray. They have already taken their trust from whatever it was on and trusted Christ alone to save them.

**Tradition is what sometimes causes confusion with our salvation.**

Walking forward in a church may be a means by which we tell someone we desire to trust Christ but walking forward in a church does not save. That is not what satisfied the wrath of God against our sin.

Signing a card may also tell someone that we wish to come to Christ. But it is trusting Christ, not the signing of a card, that saves. As I often tell people, we are saved not by doing something, but by trusting Someone.

Tradition is what sometimes causes confusion with our salvation. We see those who have walked an aisle, raised their hands at an evangelistic outreach, or signed a card. We begin associating those things with salvation. All of those may surround the *time and circumstances* through which we responded to God's free offer of eternal life, but they are not part of what constitutes salvation.

Understanding saving faith helps eliminate any doubt as to our salvation. Regardless of when and where we think we came to the Savior or even the circumstances through which we made it known we wanted to be saved, that is not where the guarantee of our salvation lies. When the Scriptures give assurance of our salvation, they always go back to a fact, not to a date or personal circumstances. What could be simpler than Christ's words in John 6:47? "Most assuredly, I say to you, he who believes in Me has everlasting life."

Some have trusted Christ at the conclusion of a church service. Others have appropriated His free gift as they drove home from church contemplating what they just heard. Others have trusted Christ as they were lying in bed for the first time being aware of His sin payment for their sin problem. Some have received the gift of eternal life sitting in their chair at the office. Still others have come to Him in a rental car or while flying to their next engagement. But when they are satisfied with the thing that satisfies God, they are forever His.

*Sometimes multitudes believed at once.*

In the New Testament we read of multitudes coming to Christ sometimes at the same moment.

"And with many other words he testified and exhorted them, saying, 'Be saved from this perverse generation.' Then those who received his word were baptized; and that day about three thousand souls were added to them." (Acts 2:40-41)

"So continuing daily with one accord in the temple, and breaking bread from house to house, they ate their food with gladness and simplicity of heart, praising God and having favor with all the people. And the Lord added to the church daily those who were being saved." (Acts 2:46-47)

"However, many of those who heard the word believed; and the number of men came to be about five thousand." (Acts 4:4)

No prayer was said, no card was signed, no aisle was walked. As they heard the gospel, they deemed it as true that Christ died for them and rose again, and were satisfied with what satisfied God as they trusted Christ alone to save them.

*Confusing phrases have hindered us.*

Sometimes the phrases we have heard in coming to Christ have caused confusion about our salvation. Although the people using this language meant well, they may not have always explained what they meant by the phrases they used. Hence, the idea of appropriating a gift and being satisfied with the thing that satisfies God was not necessarily communicated.

Even when I use the term "trust Christ," which I think is the best term to use, I explain carefully what that means. It is not trusting Him for your finances, your health, or your job, but trusting Christ alone as your only way to eternal life because He satisfied the wrath of God against your sin.

Some for example, encourage us to "accept Christ." That is the language used in one verse of the Bible when it talks about "as many as received Him." John 1:12 tells us, "But as many as received Him, to them He gave the right to become children of God, to those who believe in His name." It is interesting that the one verse that speaks the language of "accept Christ" makes it clear that the issue is believing — "even to those who believe in His name." Otherwise, we can accept Christ the way we accept one another but not be trusting in Christ to save us.

A person once said to me, "I thought you had to accept Christ in the sense of feeling He was the one He said He was. Then if you lived as good as He lived, you would get to heaven. I did not know you had to trust in Him alone to save you." It is no small wonder that he had so many doubts about his salvation and rightly so. Until he trusted Christ, he was not satisfied with the thing that satisfies God.

Others have urged, "Invite Jesus into your heart." One person that used that term sincerely meant by it that you had to appropriate His death. He explained that it is through faith in Him alone to save you that the one who is the Savior becomes *your* Savior. However, many do not explain that, so we can be led to believe that saying a prayer in which you invite Him into your heart is what saves. Nowhere does the Bible ever communicate such an idea.

That wording is usually based on Revelation 3:20. "Behold, I stand at the door and knock. If anyone hears My voice and opens the door, I will come in to him, and dine with him, and He with me." The words translated "in to" is a Greek word that actually means "toward." The issue is fellowship not entrance. Christ is speaking to a church which is lukewarm about coming closer to Him. The verse should actually not be used in inviting people to Christ. Once we trust Christ, He is already in our hearts, so there is no need to invite Him in.

Furthermore, how can one have assurance of salvation? Did He come in or did He not come in? It usually comes down to, "Do I feel Him, or do I not feel Him?" I even had a man say to me, "I was always told that you had to wait till you felt Jesus knocking at your heart and then invite Him in. I have been waiting for years to hear Him knock. I never understood that you were saved by trusting Christ alone to save you." One is saved by being satisfied with the thing that satisfies God, not by inviting Him into your heart.

Another phrase that can also be misleading and confusing as we reflect upon our salvation is "Give your life to God." That is turning the good news of the gospel backwards. There is nothing eternal about your life. Furthermore, what about the days our lives are not "given" to Him?

Salvation is not you giving God your life, but God giving you His. That is why we have eternal life. We have His life living inside of us. 1 John 5:11-12 assures us, "And this is the testimony: that God has given us eternal life, and that this life is in His Son. He who has the Son has life; he who does not have the Son of God does not have life."

Still another phrase that can confuse us is, "Give up your sin and come to Christ." We may have tried giving it up many times but sin's grip continues to hold us. Furthermore, sometimes we give it up for a month or even a year, then once again surrender to Satan's temptations. So, doubts arise about our salvation.

The issue in coming to Christ is admitting we are a sinner, not giving up our sin. Only God can help us do that. Nowhere does the Bible ever say, "Clean up your act and come to me." Instead, God urges us, "Come to Me and I will help you clean up your act." It's His divine power that comes to us through the Holy Spirit that helps us say "no" to sin and "yes" to righteous living. Hence, we can follow Paul's admonition to the church in Galatia, "If we live in the Spirit, let us also walk in the Spirit." (Galatians 5:25) Even if we fail though, we are still His children, because we have come to Christ, not because we have given up a particular sin.

## Conclusion

In inviting people to come to Christ, I always ask, "Is there anything keeping you from trusting Christ right now?" That expresses what the Bible means by *pisteuo* and invites them to be satisfied with the thing that satisfied God. Whatever phrase we use it is important that it communicates the idea, "Christ is my only way to eternal life and by faith I accept what He did on the cross in paying for my sins as my only way to heaven." Our assurance of salvation lies in the fact that God was completely satisfied that His Son's death is what atoned

> **In inviting people to come to Christ, I always ask, "Is there anything keeping you from trusting Christ right now?"**

for our sins and we are as well. We are satisfied with the thing that satisfied God. We know and believe that His sin payment completely resolved our sin problem and through personal trust in Him have appropriated His free gift of eternal life. It's simple and it's free! So simple and so free a child can understand it.

●  ●  ●

## QUESTIONS FOR REFLECTION

1.  How could you explain in eight words what the Bible means by "believe"?

2.  What is the best word that can be used today to communicate what the Bible means by "believe"?

3.  How does trusting in anyone or anything other than what Christ did on a cross demonstrate that we are not satisfied with the thing that satisfies God?

4.  Why and how is knowing the date you were saved not essential to the assurance of your salvation?

5.  How is the setting or circumstances under which you were saved unrelated to the assurance of your salvation?

6.  How can confusing phrases miscommunicate what the Bible means by "believe"?

# CHAPTER SIX

# *What exactly is repentance?*

Probably no word causes more confusion among believers and unbelievers alike than the word repentance. That confusion has caused many believers to be uncertain of their salvation. It has impacted unbelievers because when they hear the word repent they are not certain what they must do to be saved.

Genuine repentance is essential to salvation. Paul the apostle declared, "Truly these times of ignorance God overlooked, but now commands all men everywhere to repent." (Acts 17:30) What, though, does repentance mean?

*It doesn't mean to change your life.*

Repentance is often defined as a change of life. To a non-Christian that communicates that in order to come to Christ he or she must clean up their act. Take out of their lives what should not be there and put in what should be there. The problem is that would mean reformation has to come before regeneration. How does a non-Christian live the life that he has not yet been empowered to live?

It is only after a person comes to Christ that he has the ability to live a life that before he could not live.

**The problem is that would mean reformation has to come before regeneration.**

Paul's testimony was "I have been crucified with Christ; it is no longer I who live, but Christ lives in me; and the life which I now live in the flesh I live by faith in the Son of God, who loved me and gave Himself for me." (Galatians 2:20) It is only after coming to Christ that I have the supernatural power to live a supernatural life. Regeneration must precede reformation. God is not saying, "Clean up your act and then come to Me." God is saying, "Come to Me, and I will help you get your act cleaned up."

To a Christian, defining repentance as a change of life raises similar concerns. If I have to change my life, does that mean if I haven't been able to quit bad habits then I am not a Christian? How much does my life need to change to be assured I am a Christian? What about temptations I face that at times still control me instead of me controlling them? To what degree does my life need to change for me to be assured that I am a Christian? How many bad habits must I quit? What if I live splendidly one day and poorly the next? If repentance means a change of life, how would one ever be certain of salvation? How much change is enough?

*It means to change your mind.*

Repentance as used in an evangelistic context does not mean to change your life, but instead to *change your mind*. The main words used for repentance in the New Testament are the Greek words *metanoia* and *metanoeo*. They mean to change your mind about what is keeping you from trusting Christ. That is why there are different objects for the word. Sometimes it is a wrong view of God (Acts 20:21), belief in idols (Revelation 9:20), recognizing particular sins are indeed sin (Revelation 9:21), wrongful deeds one has committed (Revelation. 16:11), or a dependence on good works to save us (Hebrews 6:1). In those passages God is asking for a change of mind regarding Himself, idolatry, particular sins, deeds, and useless works.

Often the object of repentance is the person and work of Christ. For example, in Acts 2:38 we are told, "Then Peter said to them, 'Repent, and let every one of you be baptized in the name of Jesus Christ for the remission of sins; and you shall receive the gift of the Holy Spirit.'" The Jews considered Christ to be a mere man and even an impostor. They were being asked to change their minds and recognize that He was the promised Messiah, the Son of God and Savior of the world.

**What a person had to change his mind about is always determined by the context.**

What a person had to change his mind about is always determined by the context. One may have to change his wrong view of God. Another might have to change his mind about his good works, recognizing that no good thing that he does makes him acceptable to God.

What is also interesting is that sometimes the word repent is used along with the word believe, such as in Mark 1:15. "The time is fulfilled, and the kingdom of God is at hand. Repent, and believe in the gospel."

Other times it is used in place of the word believe. When Christ told a parable about lost sheep He said, "I say to you that likewise there will be more joy in heaven over one sinner who repents than over ninety-nine just persons who need no repentance." (Luke 15:7) Jesus Christ made it clear how to obtain eternal life. "Most assuredly, I say to you, he who believes in Me has everlasting life." (John 6:47) Since faith in Christ is the only means of salvation, if the angels are rejoicing over repentance, then faith in Christ must be included in that. Sometimes repent is used separate from believe and other times it is included in the word believe.

Another example of it being used as a substitute for the word believe is Acts 17:30. "Truly, these times of ignorance God overlooked, but now commands all men everywhere to repent."

### A biblical definition

*Repentance could be biblically defined as "to change your mind about what is keeping you from trusting Christ and trust Him to save you." So that means when you come to God as a sinner, recognize Christ died for you and rose again, and trust in Christ alone to save you, both faith and repentance has taken place.*

The Gospel of John was the one book of the New Testament specifically written to tell you how to receive eternal life. John 20:31 tells us, "But these are written that you may believe that Jesus is the Christ, the Son of God, and that believing you may have life in His name." Now one understands why the word "believe" is used 98 times in that book, but the word "repent" is not used once. Because when you believe in the biblical sense of the word, you have repented. You have changed your mind about whatever is keeping you from trusting Christ and trusted Him to save you. To genuinely repent is to believe in Christ as the only way to heaven.

Once we have repented, the Scriptures encourage us to bring forth fruit "befitting" repentance. In Acts 26:20, Paul said that he "declared first to those in Damascus and in Jerusalem, and throughout all the region of Judea, and then to the Gentiles, that they should repent, turn to God, and do works befitting repentance." But nowhere in Scripture is that fruit used as a determination of whether or not we are saved. We have genuinely repented when we have changed our minds about what is keeping is from trusting Christ and trusted Christ alone to save us.

## Conclusion

Repentance is essential to salvation. But when we come to God as a sinner, recognize Christ died for us and rose again, and trust Christ alone to save us, we are satisfied with what satisfies God. Both faith and repentance have taken place.

● ● ●

## QUESTIONS FOR REFLECTION

1. What does the word repentance mean and how is it related to your salvation?

2. How could a wrong view of repentance impact the assurance of your salvation?

3. How can the word "repentance" in an evangelistic context be seen as a synonym for "believe"?

# CHAPTER SEVEN

## *How does the deity of Christ impact the assurance of salvation?*

The security of the believer and the assurance we have of our salvation are interwoven with the deity of Christ. The fact that Christ is God is what secures our salvation and gives us assurance that upon trusting Christ we are forever His.

*Christ IS God.*

The Scriptures make the deity of Christ abundantly clear. He Himself claimed to be preexistent. He said, "Most assuredly, I say to you, before Abraham was, I AM." (John 8:58) He claimed equality with God by asserting that He and the Father were one. (John 5:18, 10:30) Those who heard Him had no question about what He was saying and hence accused Him of blasphemy. He claimed to be all powerful as He announced, "All authority has been given to Me in heaven and on earth." (Matthew 28:19) Even the miracles He did were designed to verify His deity and solicit faith in Him. (John 20:30-31)

Others also recognized His deity. Thomas, upon seeing the risen Christ said, "My Lord and my God!" (John 20:28) Paul, the apostle, spoke of Christ as "the eternally blessed God." (Romans 9:5) The disciples said of Him, "Truly You Are the Son of God." (Matthew 14:33) Nathaniel recognized that He had knowledge that could only come from being an all-knowing God and said of Him, "Rabbi, you are the Son of God." (John 1:48-49) Once again, the evidence throughout the Scriptures that Jesus Christ was God is abundant.

With that in mind, why and how does the deity of Christ relate to our eternal security and the assurance of our salvation? The answer is in two huge and unmistakable ways.

*Salvation is an all-powerful God holding you,*
*not you holding God.*

Salvation is not you holding God. If it was, you could never be assured of your salvation. You could possibly drop Him. At best, we are frail and weak human beings not endowed with the ability and power of the Almighty. Instead, it is God holding you.

Examine John 10:27-30. Jesus not only makes an awesome declaration, but He also repeats it two times. "My sheep hear My voice, and I know them, and they follow Me. And I give them eternal life, and they shall never perish; neither shall anyone snatch them out of My hand. My Father, who has given them to Me, is greater than all; and no one is able to snatch them out of My Father's hand. I and My Father are one."

"My sheep" is obviously a reference to believers — those who have trusted Him as their Savior. He affirms His relationship with the Father. Two times He says that absolutely nobody can snatch them out of His or His Father's Hand. The reason He gives is, "My Father, who has given them to Me, is greater than all." That means that in order to lose our salvation, we would have to be greater than God Himself. No foe of any kind can take a believer from Him.

That gives tremendous meaning to Romans 8:38-39. "For I am persuaded that neither death nor life, nor angels nor principalities nor powers, nor things present nor things to come, nor height nor depth, nor any other created thing, shall be able to separate us from the love of God which is in Christ Jesus our Lord." Paul mentions ten possibilities which encompass everyone and everything and says none of those can separate a believer from Christ.

That would even include the suicide of a believer. If suicide separated a believer from Christ, then that believer would have had to have been greater than God Himself. If a believer commits suicide, that is dishonoring to God, and will cost in terms of eternal reward, (a subject we will examine later), but in no way does he forfeit his salvation.

Some might contend: "No one can separate us from the love of God, but we *can* separate ourselves. That is, we can choose to walk away or reject God. That would clearly contradict

**Anyone or anything is powerless to take us out of His Hand.**

other verses we will examine that teach that although we can walk away for God, He never walks away from us. That would also mean that we are more powerful than the God that holds us.

Salvation is God holding us. Anyone or anything is powerless to take us out of His Hand. The God that is powerful enough to save us is powerful enough to keep us.

*A holy God cannot go back on His promises.*

You and I sometimes lie — perhaps more times than we like to admit. Hence, we fail to keep our promises. Since a holy God cannot lie, He cannot go back on His promises. Few verses say that any clearer than Romans 11:29. "For the gifts and calling of God are irrevocable." The context is the promises God made to Israel, but the application is even broader. The Scriptures are laying down a basic principle. A holy God says what He means and means what He says and does not go back on His word. "Irrevocable" has the idea He will not withdraw what He said and will not change His mind. He delivers on His promises because He is a person of holy character and integrity.

That principle is just as true as it relates to our calling unto salvation. Hence, Romans 8:30 tells us, "Moreover whom He predestined, these He also called; whom He called, these He also justified; and whom He justified, these He also glorified." A holy God has not, will not, and cannot go back on His promises. That is why Jesus could proclaim in John 6:37, "All that the Father gives Me will come to Me, and the one who comes to Me I will by no means cast out." "By no means" means just that — under no conditions and with no exceptions.

Now with that in mind, look at the repeated promises made by Jesus Christ as God's perfect Son, in relation to our salvation. Keep in mind that every promise ultimately relates to His character and integrity.

"For God so loved the world that He gave His only begotten Son, that whoever believes in Him should not perish but have everlasting life." (John 3:16)

"He who believes in Him is not condemned; but he who does not believe is condemned already, because He has not believed in the name of the only begotten Son of God." (John 3:18)

"Most assuredly, I say to you, he who hears My word and believes in Him who sent Me has everlasting life, and shall not come into judgment, but has passed from death into life." (John 5:24)

"And this is the will of Him who sent Me, that everyone who sees the Son and believes in Him may have everlasting life; and I will raise him up at the last day." (John 6:40)

"Most assuredly, I say to you, he who believes in Me has everlasting life." (John 6:47)

"Jesus said to her, 'I am the resurrection and the life. He who believes in Me, though he may die, he shall live. And whoever lives and believes in Me shall never die. Do you believe this?'" (John 11:25-26)

Now note something that is both comforting and thrilling. Neither of those — God holding us and not our holding God, nor the fact that a holy God cannot go back on His promises — have *anything* to do with our performance as a Christian, the consistency of our spiritual walk, or the extent to which our lives reflect the presence of the Savior. *Our salvation and assurance of it are centered in who He is, not who we are.* Once we come to Him, His deity and promises settle the issue. He could not even call it "eternal" life if something would happen that would cause it not to last. "Eternal" has to be "eternal." A holy God and a promise keeping God has to say what He means and mean what He says.

That is one reason I tell new believers that once you trust Christ, you then have to trust His Word. He is God! If He said it, He meant it. If He promised it, that settles it. We are His — forever — and nothing can ever change that. What proof do I have that I am the son of Paul and Miriam Moyer? It is called a birth certificate. That settles it. In essence, the Word of God is my birth certificate. He said it. That settles it!

> **If He said it, He meant it. If He promised it, that settles it.**

Even if Satan causes us to doubt our salvation, the biggest mistake we make is when we let him, so to speak, "talk to us." Satan loves to play with our mind and our emotions. He knows that if he can keep us worrying, doubting, etc., about our salvation, then we won't share our faith with others. If Satan wants to make us doubt our salvation, *his argument is with God; not with us.* If we are not saved, it is God's problem, not ours. All we did is what He told us to do — trust His Son as our only way to eternal life. We did what He told us to do, and He did what He promised to do.

> **If Satan wants to make us doubt our salvation, *his argument is with God; not with us.***

## Conclusion

An all-powerful God is holding us; we are not holding Him. God, as a holy God, is a promise keeper not a promise breaker. Those two truths alone show us how our eternal security and the assurance of it is intertwined with the deity of Christ. Being who

He is (a holy and all-powerful God) is what makes our salvation upon trusting Christ forever guaranteed. Since He is God there is no reason to doubt our salvation once we have trusted Christ. If He were not God, there would be every reason to doubt it.

● ● ●

## QUESTIONS FOR REFLECTION

1. How do the character of God and the promises of God relate to one another?

2. How is the biblical teaching that God holds us, we don't hold God, foundational to assurance of your salvation? Be specific.

3. How do the promises God makes to us versus the promises we make to God impact the assurance of our salvation?

4. Why should we direct Satan to God if he makes us struggle with our salvation and what difference would that make in terms of our assurance?

# Chapter Eight

## *So, on what basis are we assured of our salvation?*

Understanding why we struggle *before* coming to Christ may help us understand why we sometimes struggle *afterwards* with the assurance of our salvation. We have been exposed to something we have never heard or seen before — undeserved grace and unconditional love.

I have said to many, "If God said to you that to get to heaven you have to go to church three Sundays, be baptized four times, take five sacraments, and live properly for six years, you would do just that. Go to church three Sundays, be baptized four times, take five sacraments, and live properly for six years. But when God says to you, 'My Son paid for everything wrong you've done. Your entire debt has been paid. I can now give you forgiveness and eternal life completely free' you find that very difficult to accept."

*Why are grace and love so mind-boggling?*

Biblically defined, grace is undeserved favor. God gives us what we do *not* deserve and holds back from us what we *do* deserve. When it comes to love, his love is unconditional. God loves us in spite of who we are not because of who we are. Both His grace and His love are so foreign to our way of thinking. We often see God as a Santa Claus.

> **Both His grace and His love are so foreign to our way of thinking.**

We think that when we do good, we get good, and if we don't, we won't. But God is not a Santa Claus, He is a God of grace and love.

Think first about His grace. We work on the basis of debt and exchanged favors. If I invite you to join me and my wife for dinner, you are expected to invite us to join you another time. If I loan you twenty dollars, the next time I need a favor from you, you are expected to repay. I help you with a project around the house but am offended if, when I need your help, you don't return the favor.

So, grace becomes mind boggling to us. That is what makes Romans 4:4-5 so meaningful. "Now to him who works, the wages are not counted as grace but as debt. But to him who does not work but believes on Him who justifies the ungodly, his faith is accounted as righteousness." If God granted us salvation on the basis of anything we have done, or even Christ *plus* anything we have done, all He would be doing is paying a debt — giving us something He owes us. But since it is by grace, He is extending favor that we do not deserve. It is not only grace; it is amazing grace! God is not in debt to us; instead, we are in debt to God.

Now, think about His love. It is completely unconditional. It has nothing to do with who we are or what we have done. That, too, we have rarely experienced and as a result find it hard to accept. A man turns his back on a relative so the relative turns his back on him. A person goes to prison and is treated as an outcast. After all, we exclaim, "You did the crime, you do the time." The wrongs a friend has committed against us are forgiven, *as long as*, "You show me that there has been a change in your life." It is an "I love you if" kind of love, not "I love you period."

Yet what we know little of — undeserved grace and unconditional love — is intrinsic to the character of God. It comes naturally to Him; *it is who He is.* When one thinks of God, what does He think of? Holiness and power. His undeserved grace and unconditional love are as much a part of who He is as is His holiness and power. Grace and love are not a part of God, they are intrinsic to who He is. To understand grace and love at its best and at its deepest is to understand who God is. How many times do the Scriptures echo words similar to Psalm 111:4, "The Lord is gracious and full of compassion"?

Christ said to the person alongside Him as He hung on the cross, "Assuredly, I say to you, today you will be with Me in Paradise." (Luke 23:43) He was speaking to a person who deserved eternal separation

**Grace and love are not a part of God, they are intrinsic to who He is.**

from God. But he acknowledged the deity of Christ. (Luke 23:42) Christ did not accept him because he reformed his life or cleaned up his act. There was no time for any of that. He accepted him because His grace is undeserved, and His love is without any conditions of any kind.

None of us, even if we are not in our dying moments, have anything more going for us than that thief on the cross did. He sinned his way and we sin our way. God loves us because He loves us. It is just who He is. It has nothing to do with us and everything to do with Him. It is in spite of *everything* about us, not because of *anything* about us. What could be clearer or more simply stated than 1 John 4:10. "In this is love, not that we loved God, but that He loved us and sent His Son to be the propitiation for our sins."

A prime example of God's undeserved grace and unconditional love is God's working with the nation of Israel. Meditate on Ezekiel 36. Although they so often turned their backs on Him (and even had to suffer His discipline), He did not turn His back on them.

So, what makes the grace and love of God so difficult for so many to grasp is that it is something that we have not experienced from anyone anywhere. When we come to Christ, we are overwhelmed with His grace and love — and should be.

*Salvation and the assurance of it are on the same basis.*

What we sometimes miss is that the same undeserved grace and unconditional love that *saves* us also *assures* us. His character does not change once we have trusted Christ. God does not stop being who He is once we have come to Him. What was intrinsic to Him when we came to Him is also intrinsic to Him as we now walk with Him.

**God does not stop being who He is once we have come to Him.**

Because we are so accustomed to earning everything we have, sometimes we drift into thinking that although we are saved through His undeserved grace and unconditional love, we now have to do something in order to keep it or prove that we even have it. We did nothing to get it, but somehow think we have to do something to keep it. After all, isn't that how life works? *Prove* you are a good worker or the employer might tell you to clean out your desk. *Prove* you are loyal to the family or your inheritance might suffer. *Prove* you will be a good mate or your partner might leave you for somebody else. *Prove* you have been a good student or you might be looking at academic probation. Therefore, we come up with "tests" as to whether or not we are Christians.

A friend once said to me, "I'd like to have a quarter for every time I've heard people set up tests on whether a person is a Christian or not by the way they behave. If he is really a Christian, he wouldn't have done that." Usually, those tests are based on our own experiences and prejudices because in our depravity, we can be just like the legalistic Pharisees spoken of in Scripture.

If we came from an alcoholic family and were delivered from addiction, we surmise, "You cannot be a Christian and be an alcoholic." If we are annoyed by those who claim to be believers but do not go to church, we conclude, "You cannot be a Christian and not go to church." If we had a believing mate who loved us and then left us for someone else we conclude, "You cannot be a Christian and be unfaithful." If we hired a person who claimed to be a believer and then stole from our firm, we are quick to say, "I thought he was a believer, but he obviously wasn't." We even carry those "tests" into the political realm. If we are loyal to one political party and annoyed by another, we profess that one cannot be a Christian and be of the opposing party.

It would not be an overstatement to say that there have been more than 100 such "tests" given. Interestingly enough, we suggest the areas where we are strong and someone else is weak, not vice versa. That way we always come out on top. For example,

I know a believer who is extremely overweight. He is quick to use things such as sexual purity, to determine whether or not one is a believer. At the same time, he overlooks what the Bible says about a believer's need for discipline and self-control in regard to his appetite and body. (1 Corinthians 6:19-20, 9:27) So I remarked to him, "It is interesting that according to what you have just explained I cannot be a Christian if I am not in control of my sex life, but I can be a Christian if I am not in control of my appetite."

Undeserved grace and unconditional love are who God is, and that doesn't change after we come to Christ. That is why the Bible does not teach salvation by faith and assurance by works, but instead salvation by faith and assurance by faith. The basis on which we are saved is the same basis on which we are assured of our salvation. Paul rebuked the Galatians for entertaining such a thought as assurance coming from our works when he said, "Are you so foolish? Having begun in the Spirit, are you now being made perfect by the flesh?" (Galatians 3:3)

> **That is why the Bible does not teach salvation by faith and assurance by works, but instead salvation by faith and assurance by faith.**

Our salvation is based on one thing only. Have I trusted Jesus Christ and His finished work on the cross as my only way to eternal life? The assurance of our salvation is based on the same thing. Have I trusted Jesus Christ and His finished work on the cross as my only way to eternal life? Throughout Scripture, our salvation and our assurance of it is based on our justification, never on our sanctification. It is based entirely on His promises to us, not on our promises to Him.

Examine not only what the Scriptures say, but also what they do *not* say.

For example, John 6:47 has a period behind it, not a comma. "Most assuredly, I say to you, he who believes in Me has everlasting life." It does not continue, "as long as he prays like a Christian, talks like a Christian, and looks like a Christian."

John 5:24 is one of the best verses in the entire Bible on assurance. It too ends with a period not a comma. It reads, "Most assuredly, I say to you, he who hears My word and believes in Him who sent Me has everlasting life, and shall not come into judgment, but has passed from death into life." It does nor continue, "as long as his performance demonstrates him to be a Christian."

Another passage to be examined is 1 John 5:11-13. "And this is the testimony: that God has given us eternal life, and that this life is in His Son. He who has the Son has life; he who does not have the Son of God does not have life. These things I have written to you who believe in the name of the Son of God, that you may know that you have eternal life, and that you may continue to believe in the name of the Son of God."

"Know" means to know absolutely — like one knows how many fingers are on their right hand or what their address is. On what condition does one have eternal life? "He who has the Son." On what condition does one not have eternal life? "He who does not have the Son." On what condition can one know he has eternal life? "You who believe in the name of the Son of God."

The phrase "and that you may continue to believe in the name of the Son of God" has the idea that just as faith saves you, faith in Him can cause you to ask what you want of Him that is in accordance with His will knowing He will answer. Hence, verses 14-15 continue, "Now this is the confidence that we have in Him, that if we ask anything according to His will, He hears us. And if we know that He hears us, whatever we ask, we know that we have the petitions that we have asked of Him."

Salvation and the assurance of it are guaranteed on one thing — faith in the Son to save us. The Bible is clear. We are saved by faith alone and assured by faith alone. It makes sense. Anything else wouldn't be undeserved or unconditional.

But in addition to that, if salvation were by faith and assurance by works, how could we "know absolutely" (1 John 5:13) that we are saved? We would always have to ask questions such as, "Have I lived enough like a Christian?" "What about the times I have failed to pray? Does that mean I am not a believer?" "What about the areas I am strong and other Christians are weak? Does that mean I am not a Christian and they are or vice versa?" "I sometimes find the Bible a bit boring. Does that mean I am not saved?" "There are people I do not particularly enjoy or even like. Does that mean I have not been born again?" "Some of my bad habits still haunt me. Does that mean I have not trusted Christ and do not have His Spirit within me?" "I am not as consistent in church attendance as I ought to be. Does that mean I am fooling myself and I am not actually a believer?" The list of questions and struggles is almost endless. All of these verify that our focus is on ourselves instead of the finished work of Christ on the cross.

*What about the person who is not living like a Christian?*

One reason many people struggle with the simplicity of the gospel message and the assurance that accompanies it is this: how can the Holy Spirit enter a person and that person not be changed? Furthermore, they point to 2 Corinthians 5:17. "Therefore, if anyone is in Christ, he is a new creation; old things have passed away; behold, all things have become new."

That verse indeed says we are a new creation in Christ. But to use that verse to say that if anyone does not look and act like a Christian then they are not a Christian is a misuse of Scripture. I do not know of anyone who has said it better than the late Dr. Charles Ryrie. He had a big impact on me during my seminary years and I had the privilege of having lunch with him frequently. He once said, "There has to be a change, but the change may not have come on the outside yet."

If a person genuinely comes to Christ and does not grow as a Christian through talking to God in prayer, God talking to Him through the Scriptures, fellowship with other believers, and letting God day by day take out of his life what should not be there and put in what should be there, his life may not look that much different than a non-Christian's. God will do His part in salvation but we must be willing to do ours to grow. Satan loves few things more than to keep a Christian from reflecting Christ. Satan cannot do anything about a person's eternal destiny once they have trusted Christ. That was settled the moment the person came to the Savior. But he can try to keep that person from having a positive influence upon others.

In fact, if a person comes to Christ and lives in disobedience to Him, sometimes her life can be more miserable than that of an unbeliever. It's because the Holy Spirit tells her what she ought to be doing in contrast to what she is doing.

It needs to also be mentioned that a person who genuinely comes to Christ and does not move beyond his initial salvation misses out on so much God has for Him. In many ways, that person is to be pitied. Nobody can show us how to live abundantly the way He can. As He declared in John 10:10, "The thief does not come except to steal, and to kill, and to destroy. I have come that they may have life, and that they may have it more abundantly." As I have told many, knowing Christ and then growing in Him is first class living.

*Should someone not living for Christ question their salvation?*

Does that mean that a person who is not living for Christ or does not show evidence of being a Christian should not examine their salvation? Not at all. *But that cannot be the basis on which they decide whether or not they know the Lord.* If they do, they will never be sure. When is "enough" enough? There are two questions to ask in regards to where we are spiritually but they must be kept completely separate. One is, "Have I trusted Christ alone to save me?" The second is, "Am I growing and acting like a Christian?" One may have trusted Christ and yet not be growing or

**There are two questions to ask in regards to where we are spiritually but they must be kept completely separate.**

perhaps even walked away from the Lord. One may be growing (in the sense of learning more about Christ and Christian living) and acting like a Christian but has not actually trusted Christ. The good things they do and their spiritual mindedness may simply be an attempt to earn their salvation.

Even as I write this book, one of our certified instructors told me of a man he was privileged to lead to Christ using our *May I Ask You a Question?* booklet. Our instructor began following up with him and helping him grow in the Lord. During that time, the new convert was under tremendous stress at work and eventually wandered from the Lord. But although he walked away from God, God did not walk away from Him. As he faced a number of issues, the Lord convicted him of his need to come back to Him. Not only did he do so but he is now growing spiritually and regularly shares the gospel with unbelievers.

Two questions must be asked. "Have you trusted Christ alone to save you?" "Are you growing and acting like a Christian?" But keep those two questions completely separated. They are separate questions in God's mind and should be in ours.

## *Conclusion*

Thanks to undeserved grace and unconditional love, we are saved through His deity and His promises and assured of our salvation through the same. Our eternal security and the assurance of that flows from His character. Because of who He is, we are saved by faith and assured by faith. When we have trusted Christ, our salvation is forever settled in His mind and can be forever settled in ours. God's people have reason to exclaim, "Hallelujah!" As a woman who came to Christ said to me, "It's a wonderful feeling not to wonder anymore."

●  ●  ●

## QUESTIONS FOR REFLECTION

1. How is an understanding of His grace being undeserved and His love being unconditional crucial to understanding God's plan of salvation?

2. In what ways are we tempted to forget that His grace being undeserved and His love being unconditional does not change after we have trusted Christ?

3. If our assurance of salvation were on the basis of our works and performance, why would we never be certain of our salvation?

4. Why will looking at our performance not give us the assurance as to whether or not we know the Lord?

5. What two questions ought to be asked if someone is uncertain of their own salvation or the salvation of another. Why do they need to be two separate questions?

# ERRONEOUS AND
# UNBIBLICAL CONCEPTS

# CHAPTER NINE

## *What about those teachings that make us doubt our salvation?*

One reason many doubt their salvation is that things have been shared with them as biblical teachings when actually they are not biblical at all.

What are those teachings? Where do they come from and why are they in error?

*If you doubt your salvation, then you are not saved.*

The thought expressed is that if you were truly saved, you would have no reason to doubt. After all, does not 1 John 5:13 say, "These things I have written to you who believe in the name of the Son of God, that you may know that you have eternal life"? It says *know*, not doubt.

The problem with that thinking is that the person who doubts is actually questioning more than doubting (even though they may call it doubting). They are simply asking, "Am I really saved?" There is nothing wrong with that. "Doubt" (if we want to call it that) causes us to ask healthy questions. In fact, I have more concern for the person who does not ask the right question about his salvation than the one who

**In fact, I have more concern for the person who does not ask the right question about his salvation than the one who does.**

does. It is a healthy thing spiritually to ask, "Am I really saved?' and be able to say "yes" and know why and if you can't, determine why and settle the issue now.

*If you do not know the date you were saved,*
*then you are not saved.*

The idea is that you ought to know the place and the date you crossed the line from darkness into light because salvation represents a dramatic moment and is not something you can "slide into" without knowing when it happened. Some point to the example of Paul the apostle who undoubtedly could have told you the time and pointed to the place on the road to Damascus where he met the Savior. Thus, those that do not know such a date wonder, "Am I really saved?"

**Whenever Scripture gives assurance of salvation it always goes back to a fact, not to a date.**

Whenever Scripture gives assurance of salvation it always goes back to a fact, not to a date. John 6:47 does not say, "Most assuredly, I say to you, he who believes in Me and *knows the date* has everlasting life." Instead, it says, "Whoever believes in Me has everlasting life."

Some people know the date. Their conversion was so dramatic because of the background they were saved out of they can give you the moment they came to Christ. Others, particularly those raised in a God-fearing home, came to understand through a gradual process that one is saved by grace not through works. They know that they are now trusting Christ alone to save them but are not sure at what moment they crossed the line.

Emphasizing a date can be particularly harmful with children and cause them to later doubt their salvation. They may have come to Christ at an early age. But as they grow physically and spiritually, they understand God's plan of salvation better and appreciate it more. They then wonder, "Was I really saved back when I was six (or whenever)?" Parents often do them great harm by saying, "Oh yes, we know you were; we were there." The problem is if what you think happened did indeed happen, they are saved; if not, they are not saved. Who knows? Nobody can relive history. When Scripture gives assurance, it goes back to a fact not to a date. The question is: who are you trusting in *right now?* If you are trusting Christ, you are saved regardless of when you crossed the line. So instead, a parent ought to say, "Perhaps you were, perhaps you weren't. It could be that you understood as well as a child can at that age what Christ did for you on a cross. But it really does not matter. If you are trusting Christ alone to save you, you are saved regardless of when you crossed the line."

Understand that for every believer there is a specific second that they crossed from death into life. But just because a believer does not know when that second was does not mean that they are not saved. Nowhere does the Bible teach that unless one can specify the date they came to Christ, they are not saved. In fact, as I also noted earlier, I am personally convinced that there are literally thousands of believers who came to Christ earlier or later than they thought they did.

I clearly remember the night on my dad's dairy farm when I knelt by my bed and trusted Christ to save me. As far as I know that is the night I came to Christ. But when I got to Philadelphia

College of the Bible and found out that once you trust Christ you are His forever and cannot lose your salvation, I was blown away. Hence there are days I wonder, "Did I actually come to Christ that night on the dairy farm or did I come to Christ my first year of Bible college? Did I really understand that He made the complete payment for my sins and nothing could ever change that?" I think I did. But I sometimes wonder because whenever the sky looked beautiful and I thought of heaven, I reminded God again that I had trusted Christ. My answer is, I don't know and it does not matter anyway. All I know is that I am trusting Christ alone to save me and therefore I am eternally His regardless of when I crossed the line. I am eager to see Him face to face and He can then tell me the exact moment it happened.

For assurance of one's salvation, Scripture never goes back to a date but a fact. Who are you trusting in right now as your only way to eternal life? If you are trusting Christ alone, you are forever His even if you are not certain of the moment that eternal adoption into His family occurred. When you see Him face to face, just ask Him; He will be able to tell you! But even though you may not know the exact moment, it in no way means you are not saved.

*If you do not confess Him publicly, you are not saved.*

Often those who make such a statement are referring to actually walking forward before a body of believers and acknowledging that they are trusting Christ.

Put yourself in the shoes of some Christians. They may have come to Christ in the privacy of a home, at a small Bible study, through the reading of a tract, or through a conversation with a friend who witnessed to them one on one. But they have never publicly gone forward in a church and acknowledged that. To hear a statement like the above makes them wonder, "Am I truly saved?"

An evangelist was noted for saying, "There are two conditions for salvation. The one is come to Christ and the other is come forward." He was saying that both were essential for salvation.

We are immediately met with two problems. One is that means the thief on the cross to whom Christ said, "Today you shall be with Me in Paradise" (Luke 23:43) was not actually saved. How do you publicly declare Christ when you are nailed to a cross? Some might argue that he *did* confess Christ publicly because his words were recorded in Scripture. But something said to Christ personally even if it was captured in Scripture would not constitute a public profession of Christ. Secondly, John 12:42 speaks of those who genuinely came to Christ but fear kept them from acknowledging it publicly. "Nevertheless even among the rulers many believed in Him, but because of the Pharisees they did not confess Him, lest they should be put out of the synagogue."

The support for such a statement is often taken from Romans 10:9-10. "That if you confess with your mouth the Lord Jesus and believe in your heart that God has raised Him from the dead, you will be saved. For with the heart one believes unto righteousness, and with the mouth confession is made unto salvation." I personally believe that the word "saved" there is not referring to salvation from damnation, but salvation from the damages of sin in present day life. That is, if one is to live a victorious Christian life, he must be willing to confess Christ publicly. To be a silent Christian does not enable one to be a victorious Christian.

But regardless of how one interprets the word "saved," one observation makes it clear that our eternal salvation is not dependent on confessing Christ publicly. Verse ten reads, "For with the heart one believes unto righteousness." The word translated "righteousness" is the noun form of the verb translated "justifies" in Romans 4:5. "But to him who does not work but believes on Him who justifies the ungodly, his faith is accounted for righteousness." The moment we trust Christ, we are justified, meaning declared right in the sight of God. His righteousness is placed on our account — "with the heart one believes to righteousness." Our right standing before God is done with the heart, not the mouth. Confessing Christ publicly (as important as that is) has no bearing on our eternal salvation. There are also those who are sincere but shy. Walking up in front of people terrifies them.

**Our right standing before God is done with the heart, not the mouth.**

I actually had a person say to me, "I would have gone to hell before I would have gone forward." The "altar call" terrified him. I gave another kind of invitation, he trusted Christ, and so grew that he was used to lead four others to the Savior.

It is difficult to grow as a Christian if one does not openly and publicly declare that he is a Christian however and whenever God gives the opportunity. One ought to be vocal about his faith. But we are justified before God through trusting Christ to save us, not through a public confession of Christ.

*If you do not live like a Christian, then you are not a Christian.*

When people examine their lives based on a statement like that, they usually compare themselves with someone they deem to be a better Christian, which could cause them to doubt their own salvation.

The verse that is used to support that thinking (a verse so readily taken out of context) is James 2:17. "Thus also faith by itself, if it does not have works, is dead." Hence, it is concluded that if you are not living like a Christian, then you are still dead in your trespasses and sins and are without Christ.

James is speaking to people going through severe trials. They have lost their possessions and been separated from their loved ones during a time of persecution. James is fearful that during this time they might not live the life they possess. Hence, he is warning them about the danger of being a Christian with a dead faith — a faith that is not alive in good works. I sincerely think that had you said to James, "Then are you saying if a person does not have good works, he is not a Christian?" he would have said, "Where in the world did you get that idea? That is not even what I am talking about." He even calls them "brethren" and refers to their "brother or sister" which verifies that he respects them as believers. (James 2:14-15)

Even when he uses the word "saved" he is not referring to spiritual salvation, but physical, earthly, salvation. The word "saved" in Scripture simply means just that "saved". *The context has to determine the object, that which we are saved from.* Many times in Scripture it is physical salvation that is spoken of not spiritual salvation as in James 5:16 where we are told, "The prayer of faith shall save the sick." Paul, the apostle, talks about being saved from a shipwreck when he says in Acts 27:20, "Now when neither sun nor stars appeared for many days, and no small tempest beat on us, all hope that we would be saved was finally given up." It is the object of the word saved that is important. Here in chapter two of his epistle, James is talking about being saved from damage in terms of one's earthly life and testimony.

He wants them to know that during this time of hardship, it is important to not only be a Christian but to live like a Christian. We are justified before God through faith, but it is through our works that people recognize us to be who we say we are. They cannot see our heart as God does. Hence James says, "You see then that a man is justified by works, and not by faith only." (James 2:24) It is justification before men James is addressing, not justification before God. In no way is James saying that if one does not live like a Christian then they are not a Christian. He is asking a very common sense question, "What good does it do to say you have faith if you don't have works?" Furthermore, examine those in the New Testament whose lives were so shameful, yet their salvation is not questioned. The apostle Paul cites a person who was living in such gross immorality that he was going to bed with his father's wife. He says, "It is actually reported that there is sexual immorality among you, and such sexual immorality as is not even named among the Gentiles — that a man has his father's wife." (1 Corinthians 5:1) Paul was saying, "He is committing the kind of sin that even unbelievers don't commit." The fact that Paul does not doubt his salvation is seen in verse five, "Deliver such a one to Satan for the destruction of the flesh, that His Spirit may be saved in the day of the Lord Jesus."

One chapter later Paul speaks of believers who were going to court against each other. He rebukes them but does not question their salvation. "But brother goes to law against brother, and that before unbelievers!" (1 Corinthians 6:6)

Jump ahead in 1 Corinthians to chapter 11 where Paul speaks of believers whose lives were such that they were dishonoring Him by partaking of the Lord's supper. He even explains that God had to judge some of them with physical death. "For this reason many are weak and sick among you, and many sleep." (v.30)

In supporting such an emphasis as "If you don't live like a Christian, then you are not a Christian" I sometimes hear people say, "But I don't want someone to come to Christ just because they want fire insurance. I want them to live like a Christian. " Quite honestly, that is the *only* reason I came. I did not know anything about the abundant life, growing as a Christian, or living a "thank-you" life. I just knew there *was* a hell, and I did not want to go there. What we actually mean is, "I want to see people come to Christ and then live like a Christian." We all do. But let's be careful how we say that and not impose upon unbelievers things that they will only understand after they know they have been rescued from hell. The fear of hell is an excellent reason for coming to Christ.

Nowhere does the Bible teach that if one does not live like a Christian, he is not a Christian. One can walk away from the Lord just as a child can walk away from a parent. Once more, that does that mean that if one is not living like a Christian they should not ask themselves, "Am I actually a believer?" No. That is an appropriate question. But that cannot be the *basis* on which we decide if we know the Lord. The questions, "Have I trusted Christ?" and "Am I growing and living like a Christian?" are two separate questions that need to be kept separate to avoid doubts and confusion about our salvation.

> **One can walk away from the Lord just as a child can walk away from a parent.**

*If you do not love others, you are not a Christian.*

The reasoning goes, God is love. Once you come to Him you can love others the way He has loved you. If you find yourself unable to do that, then you are probably not saved.

The passage that is often used to support that thinking is 1 John 4:20-21. "If someone says, 'I love God,' and hates his brother, he is a liar; for he who does not love his brother whom he has seen, how can he love God whom he has not seen? And this commandment we have from Him: that he who loves God must love his brother also."

It needs to be noted that 1 John was written to tell us how to have fellowship with the Savior. He acknowledges that as his purpose in verses three and four of the opening chapter. "That which we have seen and heard we declare to you, that you also may have fellowship with us; and truly our fellowship is with the Father and with His Son Jesus Christ. And these things we write to you that your joy may be full."

In other words, the *Gospel of John* was written to tell us how to come to God — by believing — and uses the word "believe" 98 times. The *Epistle of 1 John* was written to tell us how to get close to the One we have come to and have intimate fellowship with Him and uses the word "abide" 24 times. You come to Christ through believing; you get close to Him through abiding.

One thing that distinguishes those who abide in Christ is the ability to love one another. It is through our closeness with Him that He teaches us how to love others the way He has loved us.

That is why 1 John 4:20 does not talk about one who *knows* God and hates his brother, but instead one who *loves* God and hates his brother. You can *know* God and hate your brother. How many Christians do you know who do? But you cannot *love* God and hate your brother. If you love the Father, you have to love the family. Even the fact that John speaks to the person who needs to love his "brother" is acknowledging the fact that both are believers.

**But you cannot *love* God and hate your brother.**

In no way is the Bible saying that if one does not love others, he is not a believer. He is begging all those who are believers to respond to others the way God has responded to us. "Beloved, if God so loved us, we ought also to love one another. (1 John 4:11)

*If there is no fruit, there is no root.*

The idea given is that if one is not bearing fruit as a believer, then it is because his faith is not rooted in Christ, and he is not actually a believer. The Scripture often used to support such thinking is Matthew 7:20. "Therefore by their fruits you will know them."

In selling real estate, salesmen are told the issue is always "location, location, location." In interpreting Scripture, the issue is always "context, context, context." The word "fruit" can mean different things in Scripture, depending on the context in which it is used. In Matthew 7, the context is false prophets. Five verses earlier Christ began, "Beware of false prophets, who come to you in sheep's clothing, but inwardly they are ravenous wolves. You will know them by their fruits. Do men gather grapes from thornbushes or figs from thistles? Even so, every good tree bears good fruit, but a bad tree bears bad fruit. Every tree that does not bear good fruit is cut down and thrown into the fire."

**In interpreting Scripture, the issue is always "context, context, context."**

The word "fruit" here does not refer to what is coming from a person's life but what is coming from their lips. Fruit refers to the false doctrine of false prophets and what it produces. What is false about them is not their works. If they did not live, act, and talk like Christians, who would believe them? They indeed wear "sheep's clothing." Their falsity is found in what they are teaching.

The Jewish audience Christ was addressing would have immediately thought of two Old Testament passages. One refers to a false prophet whose prophecy actually came to pass (Deuteronomy 13:1-5), the other to a false prophet whose prophecy was not fulfilled (Deuteronomy 18:20-22). In both situations the emphasis is not on how the prophet lived, but on what he taught. In a parallel text, Luke 6:43-45 identifies the fruit as one's words.

That is why He continues by saying, "Not everyone who says to me, 'Lord, Lord,' shall enter the kingdom of heaven, but he who does the will of My Father in heaven. Many will say to Me in that day, 'Lord. Lord, have we not prophesied in Your name, cast out demons in Your name, and done many wonders in Your name?' And then I will declare to them, 'I never knew you; depart from Me, you who practice lawlessness.'"

Note that all they did was honoring to God — prophesying, casting out demons, many wonderful works. What greater things could they do? The problem was that they were depending on those good works to give them a right standing with God. That was a false message that false prophets taught.

Instead, as Christ explained, to enter the kingdom of heaven, they had to do "the will of My Father in heaven." The "will of My Father" is defined in Christ's own words in John 6:40. "And this is the will of Him who sent Me, that everyone who sees the Son and believes in Him may have everlasting life; and I will raise him up at the last day." Receiving eternal life is not a matter of doing something but trusting someone — Jesus Christ alone — to save us.

A Christian ought to bear fruit as a believer. But just because there is no fruit does not necessarily mean there is no root and

Matthew 7:20 is certainly not teaching that. There may be any number of reasons a believer has not borne fruit — lack of growth or encouragement, not spending enough time in the Word, personal circumstances and trials, the absence of fellowship with other believers, etc.

*Carnality means that you are not a Christian.*

Such a teaching would emphasize that if one is carnal, it means he never was a Christian. In other words, a carnal Christian cannot and should not have assurance of his salvation.

**Nowhere in Scripture, though, does carnality remove the certainty of one's salvation.**

Carnality means to be governed by the flesh or by the fallen nature that resides within each person even *after* they come to Christ. That is why Paul the apostle testified, "For I know that in me (that is, in my flesh) nothing good dwells; for to will is present with me, but how to perform what is good I do not find. For the good that I will to do, I do not do; but the evil I will not do, that I practice. Now if I do what I will not to do, it is no longer I who do it, but sin that dwells in me." (Romans 7:18-20) Nowhere in Scripture, though, does carnality remove the certainty of one's salvation. There is probably no paragraph in Scripture that makes that any clearer than 1 Corinthians 3:1-4 — a passage that makes it clear that a person can be carnal and yet be a genuine believer.

"And I, brethren, could not speak to you as to spiritual people but as to carnal, as to babes in Christ. I fed you with milk, and not with solid food; for until now you were not able to receive it, and even now you are still not able; for you are still carnal. For where there are envy, strife, and divisions among you, are you not carnal and behaving like mere men? For when one says, 'I am of Paul,' and another, 'I am of Apollos,' are you not carnal?"

The fact that Paul calls them "brethren" means he regards them as genuine believers — a salutation which never includes unregenerate people. They are simply babes in Christ — a term which in itself indicates the security they can have that they are believers. Their spirituality though is lacking such depth that they cannot receive the strong meat of the Word but only the "milk." This carnality was seen in their proneness to emphasize human leaders and overlook the fact that we are all one in the body of Christ and of equal importance to Him.

Can a person be acting in a carnal way because he has never come to Christ? Of course! That is why the two questions mentioned earlier must be kept separate — (1) Have I trusted Christ alone to save me and (2) Am I growing and acting like a Christian? But if we have sincerely trusted Christ, being carnal as a believer does not erode our eternal security or the assurance we can have that we are His. We ought, though, to take our carnality seriously and so progress spiritually that we can receive the meat of the Word.

## Conclusion

Whenever we hear anything, we ought to do what the people of Berea did in Acts 17:11 as they listened to Paul and Silas. We are told "...they received the word with all readiness, and searched the Scriptures daily to find out whether these things were so."

When one asks of the above beliefs, "Is that what the Bible teaches?" the answer is a resounding "No." They are simply statements or sayings that our enemy Satan wants to use to take away the assurance of our salvation. Few things irritate our enemy more than for a believer to walk through life with the thrill of knowing that once he belongs to God, nothing can change that.

● ● ●

## QUESTIONS FOR REFLECTION

1. What should a person do if he has doubts about his salvation?

2. Why is it not essential to know the date you were saved?

3. Why is confessing Christ publicly not a condition of salvation?

4. Where in the New Testament are there instances of believers whose lives were not always lived in obedience to Christ?

5. What is different about the purpose of the Gospel of John and the epistle of 1 John and how is that evidenced?

# Understanding Difficult Paragraphs

# CHAPTER TEN

## *Paragraphs that might confuse us*

If not interpreted in context, many paragraphs of Scripture can cause one to question if he or she is saved. A few (if not understood properly) might even cause some to wonder if God doesn't *encourage* us to doubt our salvation. If understood properly though, instead of taking away from the security and assurance of our salvation, these passages contribute to it.

Before looking at these paragraphs, one thing must be emphasized. The Bible does not contradict itself. Therefore, it is a principle of biblical interpretation that you always allow the clear to interpret the unclear.

For example, there are six verses in the Bible that *appear* to teach that baptism saves (giving the impression that unless one is baptized he does not receive eternal life). However, more than 100 verses very clearly state that you are saved through faith alone. The clear always has to interpret the unclear. So whatever those six verses are saying, it does not change the fact that one is saved by faith alone in Christ alone. Baptism has no saving value. It is simply the first step of discipleship after a person has trusted Christ. When one looks at those six verses with that understood, he finds an alternate explanation of those verses in their proper context. That interpretation reveals that those verses are saying something other than teaching that baptism saves.

Likewise, in examining paragraphs that could cause one to question his or her salvation, the clear must interpret the unclear. The passages that teach one is forever secure upon faith in a risen Savior are unmistakable and abundant.

But where are those paragraphs that cause some to question their salvation, and why do they not need to confuse us?

*What about the parable of the sower and the seed?*

Some are inclined to think that there is no salvation unless there is growth in our lives. Let's first look at the parable and then the Lord's explanation of it.

"A sower went out to sow his seed. And as he sowed, some fell by the wayside; and it was trampled down, and the birds of the air devoured it. Some fell on rock; and as soon as it sprung up, it withered away because it lacked moisture. And some fell among thorns, and the thorns sprang up with it and choked it. But others fell on good ground, sprang up, and yielded a crop a hundredfold." (Luke 8:5-8)

"Now the parable is this: The seed is the word of God. Those by the wayside are the ones who hear; then the devil comes and takes away the word out of their hearts, lest they should believe and be saved. But the ones on the rock are those who, when they hear, receive the word with joy; and they have no root, who believe for a while and in time of temptation fall away. Now the ones that fell among thorns are those who, when they have heard, go out and are choked with cares, riches, and pleasures of life, and bring no fruit to maturity. But the ones that fell on good ground are those who, having heard the word with a noble and good heart, keep it and bear fruit with patience." (Luke 8:11-15)

Several observations. In general, parables were always designed to teach a simple truth (similar to when a speaker uses an illustration) because that is what the parables were — illustrations to drive home biblical truth. To pick the parables apart instead of grasping the "big idea" of each parable is to miss the point Christ was making.

**To pick the parables apart instead of grasping the "big idea" of each parable is to miss the point Christ was making.**

Here the simple truth being taught is that the reason there are different responses to the Scriptures is because of the *difference in the soil not the seed* (meaning the Word of God). People's hearts differ and hence there are different responses. Nothing more would need to be said. To use the details of the parable and analyze the characters is to miss the purpose and point of the passage. Do not read more into a parable than what Jesus was teaching.

That being said, though, it is worth noting that in every soil but the first who is declared an unbeliever ("lest they should believe and be saved") new life did result. Therefore, the remaining three could be assumed to be believers. The second seed which fell upon rock fell away because of not being rooted enough to withstand temptation. The third, that which fell among thorns, failed to reach maturity because of being choked out with the cares, riches, and pleasures of life. The fourth is what you wish every believer would be — one who receives the Word, bears fruit, grows and keeps on growing.

Hence, to use this parable to question one's salvation is not the proper use of Scripture, missing the main point being told. Furthermore, even if one does apply the details in that manner, the last three are believers in differing places in their spiritual walk and growth.

*Doesn't John 15:6 teach that God could cast us out if we are unfruitful meaning we are no longer saved or were not saved to begin with?*

This verse is set in the context of discipleship, not salvation.

"If anyone does not abide in Me, he is cast out as a branch and is withered; and they gather them and throw them into the fire, and they are burned."

Note that Jesus is addressing His disciples. (John 13:1,23) Seven times within the first eight verses of John 15 the word "abide" appears which, as we have discussed and will mention again, has to do with fellowship with Christ, not salvation.

The paragraph talks about the process of pruning. Dead wood is cut away. The branches that are bearing fruit are cut back so that clusters of grapes may be rich and full. The branches have to be able to draw sap from the vine.

Christ desires that we be fruitful. Two verses later He says, "By this My Father is glorified, that you bear much fruit; so you will be My disciples." It is only when we abide in Christ that we are fruitful as we draw from His strength not from ours. Disciples who do not abide in Him can suffer divine discipline to move them toward fruitfulness. He says in verse two, "Every branch in Me that does not bear fruit He takes away; and every branch that bears fruit He prunes, that it may bear

**It is only when we abide in Christ that we are fruitful as we draw from His strength not from ours.**

more fruit." Since the context is discipleship, "fire" here must be taken as a portrayal of this divine discipline, not the literal fires of hell. Note the progression. There is the loss of fellowship ("he is cast out as a branch"), the loss of spiritual vitality ("and is withered"), and divine discipline ("they gather them and throw them into the fire, and they are burned").

Those that are fruitful have the opposite experience. In verse two He said, "Every branch that bears fruit He prunes, that it may bear more fruit." The Greek word for "prune" means to "make clean." Laborers in the vineyards would have to wash from the branches deposits made by insects, moss, and other parasites that could hinder fruitfulness. God uses the Word in our lives to clean us of things that would hinder our fruitfulness. That is why He said in verse three, "You are already clean because of the word which I have spoken to you."

Christ is in no way causing a believer to doubt his salvation but instead He is reminding us how important abiding in Him is to fruitfulness. He so strongly stated, "Without Me, you can do nothing." (v.5)

*If we cannot lose our salvation, why does Paul the apostle*
*tell some, "You have fallen from grace"?*

After Paul preached the gospel of grace, some with a legalistic mindset tried to pervert that message (Galatians 1:7). They attempted to teach that along with faith in Christ one needed to keep the law and be circumcised to be right with God. Paul begins in chapter five, verse one by urging them, "Stand fast therefore in the liberty by which Christ has made us free, and do not be entangled again with the yoke of bondage." He even explained that if one were to keep the law, he would have to keep the whole law. (v.3) It is then he says, "You have become estranged from Christ. You who attempt to be justified by law; you have fallen from grace." (v.4)

**He is not talking about the loss of salvation but leaving a grace approach for an approach to living the Christian life that will not effectively deliver them from sin's influence in everyday life.**

Paul's point is that since it is impossible to be justified by any good deeds on our part such as keeping the law, to even endorse such thinking is to abandon or fall away from the gospel of grace. He is not talking about the loss of salvation but leaving a grace approach for an approach to living the Christian life that will not effectively deliver them from sin's influence in everyday life. An analogy would be when a believer leaves a church that teaches salvation by grace and joins one that teaches that salvation depends on something we have done (such as good works, baptism, and church attendance) instead of what Christ has done for us. Such a believer has not lost his salvation but has "fallen from grace." He has left a grace approach to salvation.

*Doesn't Colossians 1:21-23 teach that we have to
continue in the faith to be saved?*

Upon reading this passage, some would surmise that a person only knows they are going to heaven if they "continue in the faith."

"And you, who once were alienated and enemies in your mind by wicked works, yet now has He reconciled in the body of His flesh through death, to present you holy, and blameless, and above reproach in His sight — if indeed you continue in the faith, grounded and steadfast, and are not moved away from the hope of the gospel which you heard, which was preached to every creature under heaven, of which, I, Paul, became a minister."

Paul clearly stated that the believers in Colossae were reconciled to Christ through His death so that He might present them "holy, and blameless, and above reproach in His sight." He did not want them to stop at conversion. Instead, he wanted them to come to maturity and lead holy lives. Five verses later he explains, "Him we preach, warning every man and teaching every man in all wisdom, that we may present every man perfect in Christ Jesus."

The Greek word for "perfect" means "mature". Only if they go past their conversion and grow to maturity will they be prepared to stand before God as holy, blameless, and beyond reproach in His sight. He wants them to be blameless in the way he admonished church leaders to be in 1 Timothy 3:2. "A bishop then must be

**We are now urged to grow to maturity, cling to the gospel that saved us, and remain steadfast so that one day we can stand before Him with lives that are well pleasing to Him.**

blameless, the husband of one wife, temperate, sober-minded, of good behavior, hospitable, able to teach."

That will only happen if they "continue in the faith, grounded and steadfast, and are not moved away from the hope of the gospel." Their ears must be closed to false teachers as they remain steadfast in the truth of the gospel.

Instead of teaching that we are only saved if we continue in the faith, this verse assures us that we are reconciled to God through His death on the cross. Our salvation is settled. We are now urged to grow to maturity, cling to the gospel that saved us, and remain steadfast so that one day we can stand before Him with lives that are well pleasing to Him.

*Doesn't 1 Corinthians 6:9-10 warn us that if we practice certain vile sins we may lose our salvation or may have never had it?*

As Paul writes to the Corinthians he tells them, "Do you not know that the unrighteous will not inherit the kingdom of God? Do not be deceived. Neither fornicators, not idolaters, nor adulterers, not homosexuals, nor sodomites, nor thieves, nor covetous, nor drunkards, nor revilers, nor extortioners will inherit the kingdom of God."

First, since the word "inherit" is sometimes used in Scripture to speak of rewards (Colossians 3:24, 2 Timothy 2:11-13), it could be argued that Paul is saying that those believers who practice such vile sins will lose eternal rewards in the eternal kingdom. All believers get to heaven, but it is the faithful ones that are rewarded (as will later be discussed).

In light of the context, the more probable explanation, is that Paul is simply telling the believers not to act like unbelievers. In the previous paragraph, he rebukes them as believers for going to court against each other and suing one another. In verses six and seven he says, "But brother goes to law against brother, and that before unbelievers! Now therefore, it is already an utter failure for you that you go to law against one another. Why do you not rather accept wrong? Why do you not rather let yourselves be cheated?" Then, in the following verse he says, "And such were some of you. But you were washed, but you were sanctified, but you were justified in the name of the Lord Jesus and by the Spirit of God."

> **In light of the context, the more probable explanation, is that Paul is simply telling the believers not to act like unbelievers.**

In no way is he saying that they were never saved. Nor is he saying that they lost their salvation. He is naming some things non-Christians who will not even enter the kingdom often do (that should be no part of the life of a believer), including going to court against each other.

*Since 1 Corinthians 9:27 teaches that we could become*
*"disqualified," doesn't that mean we could lose our salvation?*

Sometimes a single word in a verse can cause one to jump to wrong conclusions and misunderstand its meaning unless one reads the entire paragraph. In this case, it's the paragraph in which "disqualified" is found that enables one to understand Paul's use of the word.

**Having encouraged others to endure and be used of the Lord, Paul wants to so discipline himself that he does not become disapproved and lose reward.**

"Do you not know that those who run in a race all run, but one receives the prize? Run in such a way that you may obtain it. And everyone competes for the prize is temperate in all things. Now they do it to obtain a perishable crown, but we for an imperishable crown. Therefore I run thus: not with uncertainty. Thus I fight: not as one who beats the air. But I discipline my body and bring it into subjection, lest, when I have preached to others, I myself should become disqualified." (1 Corinthians 9:24-27)

The Greek word "disqualified" has the idea "disapproved after testing." The words "prize" and "crown" represent the reward one receives for being willing to suffer and endure in the name and for the sake of Christ. Based on the context, some of that reward may be the reward of being used to lead others to Jesus. In verse 22 he stated, "I have become all things to all men, that I might by all means save some." Having encouraged others to endure and be used of the Lord, Paul wants to so discipline himself that he does not become disapproved and lose reward.

The paragraph is challenging believers to steadfastness and endurance, not in any way threatening them with the possible loss of their salvation.

*Doesn't 2 Corinthians say, "Examine yourselves as to whether you are in the faith"?*

If not understood properly, this passage can easily be taken to mean "You better look at yourself. You might not be a Christian after all." A key passage used to suggest this is 2 Corinthians 13:5.

"Examine yourselves as to whether you are in the faith. Test yourselves. Do you not know yourselves, that Jesus Christ is in you? — unless indeed you are disqualified."

Was he not admonishing them to look at their lives to determine if they were truly saved?

What makes that doubtful is that in his first letter to them he addressed them as "those who are sanctified in Christ Jesus, "enriched in everything by Him in all utterance and all knowledge," "eagerly waiting for the revelation of our Lord Jesus Christ," and "called into the fellowship of His Son, Jesus Christ our Lord." (1 Corinthians 1:2,5,7,9)

**Once again, the context solves the problem and gives the proper meaning to the text.**

Once again, the context solves the problem and gives the proper meaning to the text. Paul is placed on the defensive. The Corinthians were challenging Paul's authority. Two verses earlier in 2 Corinthians 13 he said, "You seek a proof of Christ speaking in me." One chapter earlier he had to remind them of the proofs of his apostleship (12:12) and agonized over the fact that the more he loved them, the less they loved him (12:15).

What he is saying here is, "Examine yourselves instead of me!" He said, "Do you not know yourselves, that Jesus Christ is in you? — unless indeed you are disqualified." The word disqualified doesn't mean "unless you are not a Christian." It means "being disapproved." It is a word Paul used of himself in the area of being rewarded for faithful service. "But I discipline my body and bring it into subjection, lest, when I have preached to others, I myself should become disqualified." (1 Corinthians 9:27)

Paul is not questioning their salvation. Instead, he is expressing the need to live a God-honoring life that manifests Christ working in and through them. In so doing, they will not be disapproved in terms of meriting eternal reward. In light of all the "contentions, jealousies, outbursts of wrath, selfish ambitions, backbitings, whisperings, conceits, tumults…uncleanness, fornication, and lewdness" that existed within Corinthian church. That was certainly a needed warning (2 Corinthians 12:20-21). In no way, though, is he encouraging them to doubt their salvation.

*Doesn't Hebrews 3:12-14 encourage one to doubt their salvation or even present the possibility of forfeiting your salvation?*

Several passages in the book of Hebrews cause some to wonder if unless certain conditions are met, one should doubt their salvation. Hebrews 3:12-14 is certainly one of them. Again, let's look at the passage.

"Beware, brethren, lest there be in any of you an evil heart of unbelief in departing from the living God; but exhort one another daily, while it is called 'Today,' lest any of you be hardened through the deceitfulness of sin. For we have become partakers of Christ if we hold the beginning of our confidence steadfast to the end."

Doesn't "if we hold the beginning of our confidence steadfast to the end" cause one's salvation and the assurance of it to be "iffy?"

The context of these verses is Israel's failure that resulted in 40 years of wandering in the wilderness (3:7-11). The writer of Hebrews wanted his readers to guard against the hard-heartedness that characterized the Israelites in the wilderness. Hence, he says, "exhort one another daily ... lest any of you be hardened through the deceitfulness of sin."

**The privilege of ruling with Christ in His future kingdom involves holding on to our confidence and hope to the end.**

"Partakers with Christ" could be translated "partners with Christ." What the writer means by being partners with Christ, the messianic King, is seen by dropping back to verses five and six of the same chapter. "And Moses indeed was faithful in all His house as a servant, for a testimony of those things which would be spoken of afterward, but Christ as the Son over His own house, whose house we are if we hold fast the confidence and rejoicing of the hope firm to the end."

Moses was faithful in exercising his responsibilities within the tabernacle which was but a shadow over the house where Christ presides. Believers likewise share in His dominion over the created order which Christ will forever rule. The privilege of ruling with Christ in His future kingdom involves holding on to our confidence and hope to the end.

In no way is the writer of Hebrews doubting their salvation nor is he encouraging them to doubt it. He is simply stating that the privilege of serving with Christ and in some way ruling with Him is based on remaining faithful to Him. A similar thought is expressed in Revelation 2:26-27. "And he who overcomes, and keeps My works until the end, to him I give power over the nations — He shall rule them with a rod of iron..."

*Isn't it possible, in light of Hebrews 6:4-6 to "taste"*
*salvation, but not actually have it?*

Ironically, a paragraph that assures us of our salvation has caused some to doubt theirs.

"For it is impossible for those who were once enlightened, and have tasted of the heavenly gift, and have become partakers of the Holy Spirit, and have tasted the good word of God and the powers to come, if they fall away, to renew them again to repentance, since they crucify again for themselves the Son of God, and put Him to an open shame."

Three words need to be noted. The word *tasted* is the same Greek word used for Christ in Hebrews 2:9. "But we see Jesus, who was made a little lower than the angels, for the suffering of death crowned with glory and honor that He, by the grace of God, might taste death for every man." In "tasting" death, Christ did not come close to dying; He actually died. "Tasted" was an established idiom for the experience of knowing the Lord. Peter says, "As newborn babes, desire the pure milk of the word, that you may grow thereby, if indeed you have tasted that the Lord is gracious." (1 Peter 2:2-3)

The word *enlightened* is the same word translated "illuminated" in Hebrews 10:32 to describe the readers' genuine conversion experience. "But recall the former days in which, after you were illuminated, you endured a great struggle with sufferings."

*Partakers* is used to speak to believers about their heavenly calling in Hebrews 3:1, even calling them "holy brethren." "Therefore, holy brethren, partakers of the heavenly calling, consider the Apostle and High Priest of our confession, Christ Jesus."

Believers are in view in Hebrews 6:4-6. The author portrays a believer who has strayed from the Lord. This fits the theme of Hebrews which is "We cannot go back; we must go on" since it is written to those could waiver in their walk with the Lord in the same way the Israelites did in the wilderness. Just three verses later the writer said, "But, beloved, we are confident of better things concerning you, yes, things that accompany salvation, though we speak in this manner. For God is not unjust to forget your work and labor of love which you have shown toward His name, in that you have ministered to the saints, and do minister. And we desire that each one of you show the same diligence to the full assurance of hope until the end, that you do not become sluggish, but imitate those who through faith and patience inherit the promises."

The passage portrays a Christian who wanders so far from God that it is impossible to renew him to repentance — to bring him to a change of mind. First John 5:16 -17 warns of that possibility when it says, "If anyone sees his brother sinning a sin which does not lead to death. He will ask, and He will give him life for those who commit sin not leading to death. There is sin leading to death. I do not say that he should pray about that." A Christian who so strays from God may face the danger of divine judgment as God disciplines him with physical death.

**It is never a light thing to stray from God.** Why is such judgment necessary? Because Christians who so stray from God "crucify again for themselves the Son of God and put Him to an open shame." They approach Christ the way that those who crucified Him did and expose Christ to public shame. Since they are believers, they invite God's judgment upon their lives. The writer of Hebrews does not specify what form the discipline may take, whether it be sickness, death, or hardships of any kind. It simply warns of the danger of discipline because of the way they are dishonoring His name. As my mentor Haddon Robinson one time said, "If a man fails to walk with God, he walks on the edge of an abyss." It is never a light thing to stray from God. In verses seven and eight he even gives an analogy they could identify with — the burning of a field to destroy unfruitful growth so that fruitfulness could begin.

Instead of doubting their salvation, security, and assurance, the writer drives home the severity of walking away from the Lord. The danger spoken of is discipline, not damnation. But he encourages them "We are confident of better things concerning you" (v.9). Such a warning ought to cause all of us to do what he began this discussion with "go on to perfection." (v.1)

*If salvation is a guarantee, why does Hebrews 12:14 teach that holiness is necessary to see the Lord?*

Hebrews 12:14 causes some to doubt their salvation and others to question if they can keep it.

"Pursue peace with all people, and holiness, without which no one will see the Lord."

Once more, examine the context! The writer is talking to believers about the purpose and benefit of being disciplined by the Lord. "If you endure chastening, God deals with you as with sons; for what son is there whom a father does not chasten? (v.7)

"Now no chastening seems to be joyful for the present, but painful; nevertheless, afterward it yields the peaceable fruit of righteousness to those who have been trained by it." (v.11) He even encouraged them to help strengthen weaker Christians. "Therefore strengthen the hands which hang down, and the feeble knees, and make straight paths for your feet, so that what is lame may not be dislocated, but rather be healed." (vv.12-13)

**In light of the fact that he is speaking to believers, there are two ways to interpret Hebrews 12:14.**

One way of encouraging one another and keeping ourselves spiritually vibrant is by "pursuing peace with all people, and holiness, without which no one will see the Lord." In light of the fact that he is speaking to believers, there are two ways to interpret Hebrews 12:14.

One is that when we as believers are in God's presence, we will be as holy as He is holy — "we shall be like Him." (1 John 3:2) Awareness of that ought to cause us to want to be as holy as He is now. Second, it is those who have pure and holy lives who have the best perception and understanding of God's will and the way He wants to work in and through them. It is a similar idea to Matthew 5:8. "Blessed are the pure in heart, for they shall see God." The pure in heart are those who recognize their justified condition before God and wish to be pure in their walk with Him.

No question about their salvation is in view. There is simply a challenge to keep their spiritual lives vibrant so that they do not fall short of what God in His grace has for them. He wants them to "serve God acceptably with reverence and godly fear." (Heb. 12:28)

*Doesn't the book of Revelation warn us about the danger of having our name blotted out of the Book of Life?*

Two passages in Revelation cause readers concern that perhaps eternal life is not as guaranteed as other passages insist it is. The fact is that they are easily explained and say the opposite. One is Revelation 3:5 which contains the phrase "blot out his name from the Book of Life."

"He who overcomes shall be clothed in white garments, and I will not blot out his name from the Book of Life; but I will confess his name before My Father and before His angels."

"Blot out" is a figure of speech in which the positive is affirmed by negating what is negative. It is a way of saying, "This will happen, and this will most certainly not happen." The passage is not stating that *any* believer will have his name blotted out of the Book of Life, which contains the name of those who are forever His. It is simply affirming that believers who are faithful will be most certainly rewarded as the Lord publicly confesses their names and speaks of their faithfulness. They are His and also most certainly their names will not be blotted out of the Book of Life.

**Instead of causing one to question their salvation, Revelation 3:5 affirms it.**

An analogy may help. Suppose I said, "Anyone who enters my house will receive a warm welcome, will dine at my table, and most certainly will never be asked to leave." I am affirming the positive by negating what is negative. The fact is that *anyone* who enters my house will not be asked to leave and most certainly those who dine at my table.

Instead of causing one to question their salvation, Revelation 3:5 affirms it. No believer's name will be blotted out of the Book of Life.

*So, what does Revelation 3:16 mean when it says,*
*"I will vomit you out of My mouth"?*

The first part of this sentence is what gives meaning to the phrase.

"So then, because you are lukewarm, and neither cold nor hot, I will vomit you out of My mouth."

**God was using such a vivid analogy to stress how distasteful the believers of Laodicea were.** Cold water is refreshing and hot water can serve a multitude of purposes. But lukewarm water is distasteful. God was using such a vivid analogy to stress how distasteful the believers of Laodicea were. Their emphasis was on their wealth instead of their spiritually pathetic condition. They were so distasteful that He felt like vomiting them out of His mouth.

The verse is not addressing their salvation but how spiritually self-deluded they were as believers and how distasteful their lives had become.

## Conclusion

Context! Context! Context! When one carefully studies the Scriptures he discovers that these admittedly difficult passages are in no way taking away from the biblical teaching that we are saved by faith and assured by faith. Examining the clear against the unclear, and examining these passages in their proper context, gives needed and proper instruction in Christian living. In no way were they written to make us question our salvation.

● ● ●

## Questions for Reflection

1. How is the principle that "the clear must interpret the unclear" foundational to biblical interpretation?

2. Why is handling the Bible in context essential to being assured of one's salvation?

3. In what way do the Scriptures properly interpreted contribute to assurance of our salvation instead of causing us to doubt our salvation?

# BIBLICAL DISTINCTIONS

# CHAPTER ELEVEN

## *Entering the christian life versus living the christian life*

One way believers bring confusion into their own lives (especially regarding their salvation) is when they confuse entering the Christian life with living the Christian life. Likewise, unbelievers can also misunderstand when that distinction is not made clear. Whereas entering the Christian life is very simple and easy, living the Christian life can sometimes become very difficult and complex.

First, we enter it.

Entering the Christian life is easy because eternal life is free. Yet, while it is free to us, it cost God everything. He had to let His own Son take the punishment we deserved so He could treat us as though we have never sinned. 2 Corinthians 5:21 tells us, "For He made Him who knew no sin to be sin for us, that we might become the righteousness of God in Him."

**Saying eternal life is free does not mean it's cheap.**

Saying eternal life is free does not mean it's cheap. It simply means that the greatest price one could have to pay, the death of His own Son on a cross, has already been paid. Jesus Christ paid it when He died as our substitute. Eternal life is anything but cheap. It cost God His own Son.

That is one reason it is so humbling to come to Christ. The apostle Paul reminded the Corinthians, "For you see your calling, brethren, that not many wise according to the flesh, not may mighty, not many noble, are called. But God has chosen the foolish things of the world to put to shame the wise, and God has chosen the weak things of the world to put to shame the things which are mighty; and the base things of the world and the things which are despised God has chosen, and the things which are not, to bring to nothing the things that are, that no flesh should glory in His presence." (1 Corinthians 1:26-29)

Paul's point was that more lower class people came to Christ than those from the upper class. The powerful and highly educated took pride in their achievements and that often kept them from seeing their need and accepting something that they could not earn.

Nothing we are, nothing we do, and nothing we would promise to do makes us deserve that gift. In fact, to even offer any of that to God in an attempt to earn our salvation is an insult to His grace.

I have told thousands that I could understand why anyone would not come to Christ if he had to clean up his act, go to church for five years, keep most of the Ten Commandments, be baptized, take the sacraments offered by the church, or promise to live an exemplary life for a minimum of ten years. But for the life of me, I do not understand why anyone would turn down a free gift — especially one that results in eternity in the presence of God Himself.

Actually though, I do know why. Coming to Christ is a humbling experience. Nothing we are or do makes us deserve God's free gift.

Furthermore, there are no strings attached. God never attaches an "if" to His offer — if you pray like you should, read the Bible like you should, treat others like you should, etc. If He did, it would not be unconditional love. Genuine unconditional love has no strings attached. What could be simpler than one of the best known verses of the Bible — John 3:16. "For God so loved the world that He gave His only begotten Son, that whoever believes in Him should not perish but have everlasting life."

> **God never attaches an "if" to His offer — if you pray like you should, read the Bible like you should, treat others like you should, etc.**

We receive that gift by trusting Christ alone to save us. As has been stated earlier, at that point we are satisfied with the thing that satisfied God. A divine transaction takes place. Romans 4:5 explains, "But to him who does not work but believes on Him who justifies the ungodly, his faith is accounted for righteousness." The word "accounted" means God takes our sins from our account and places them on Christ's account where they were paid for through the cross. He takes His Son's righteousness and places it on our account. So, when He looks upon us, He no longer sees our sin but instead the perfection of His Son Jesus. We are not *made* righteous because there is no way, as sinners, we could be. We are *declared* righteous.

That is another reason we cannot lose our salvation. God would have to "undo" a divine transaction. He would have to take our sins from Christ's account and place those back on us and take

His Son's righteousness from our account and place that back on Christ. Furthermore, if salvation cannot be earned by good deeds (as Romans 4:5 states), it cannot be lost by bad deeds.

How could entering the Christian life be any simpler than that? And the more one ponders that upon coming to Christ, the more he wants to live for the One who died for him out of an attitude of gratitude. "And He died for all, that those who live should live no longer for themselves, but for Him who died for them and rose again." (2 Corinthians 5:15) The greatest gift one could ever get is received freely because of the unconditional love and grace of God — and it's available to anyone anywhere!

*After we enter it, then we live it.*

The Scriptures make a clear distinction between entering the Christian life and living it. Many lengthy passages could be cited. Let me address two. A simple reading of these two passages would cause even the casual reader of Scripture to say, "He is talking about how to live the Christian life, not how to enter it."

A prime example is Colossians 3:1-10. We are told, "If then you were raised with Christ, seek those things which are above, where Christ is, sitting at the right hand of God. Set your mind on things above, not on things on the earth. For you died, and your life is hidden with Christ in God. When Christ who is our life appears, then you also will appear with Him in glory. Therefore put to death your members which

**The Scriptures make a clear distinction between entering the Christian life and living it.**

are on the earth: fornication, uncleanness, passion, evil desire, and covetousness, which is idolatry. Because of these things the wrath of God is coming upon the sons of disobedience, in which you yourselves once walked when you lived in them. But now you yourselves are to put off all these: anger, wrath, malice, blasphemy, filthy language out of your mouth. Do not lie one to another, since you have put off the old man with his deeds, and have put on the new man who is renewed in knowledge according to the image of Him who created him."

Now examine Ephesians 4:17-32. We read, "This I say, therefore, and testify in the Lord, that you should no longer walk as the rest of the Gentiles walk, in the futility of their mind, having their understanding darkened, being alienated from the life of God, because of the ignorance that is in them, because of the blindness of their heart; who, being past feeling, have given themselves over to lewdness, to work all uncleanness with greediness. But you have not so learned Christ. If indeed you have heard Him and have been taught by Him, as the truth is in Jesus: that you put off, concerning your former conduct, the old man which grows corrupt according to the deceitful lusts, and be renewed in the spirit of your mind, and that you put on the new man which was created according to God, in true righteousness and holiness. Therefore, putting away lying, "Let each one of you speak truth with his neighbor," for we are members of one another. "Be angry and do not sin," do not let the sun go down on your wrath, nor give place to the devil. Let him who stole steal no longer, but rather let him labor, working with his hands what is good, that he may have something to give him who has need. Let no corrupt word proceed out of your mouth, but what is good for necessary edification, that it may impart grace to the hearers. And do not grieve the Holy Spirit of God, by whom you were sealed for the day of redemption. Let all bitterness, wrath, anger, clamor, and evil speaking be put away form you, with all malice. And be kind to one another, tenderhearted, forgiving one another, even as God in Christ forgave you."

Whereas entering the Christian life is simple and easy, living the Christian life can be very difficult and complex. Those passages make it clear that one could be a believer and although he ought not, still be a fornicator, have uncontrolled anger, use filthy language, lie to someone, or steal from someone. The Scriptures even warn us that a believer will often face struggles and temptations in the areas of the lust of the flesh, the lust of the eyes, and the pride of life. (1 John 2:16)

> **Whereas entering the Christian life is simple and easy, living the Christian life can be very difficult and complex.**

The believers in the Corinthian church were at times everything but what believers ought to be. Paul rebuked them for that and his letter to them that we refer to as 2 Corinthians speaks to them about some of the specific things going on in their assembly. "For I fear lest, when I come, I shall not find you such as I wish, and that I shall be found by you such as you do not wish; lest there be contentions, jealousies, outbursts of wrath, selfish ambitions, backbitings, whisperings, conceits, tumults; lest when I come again, my God will humble me among you, and I shall mourn for many who have sinned before and have not repented of the uncleanness, fornication, and lewdness which they have practiced." (2 Corinthians 12:20-21)

That is why confusing the two — entering the Christian life and living the Christian life — can cause confusion in understanding eternal security and assurance of salvation.

Let's look at that from another direction. Examine five things that Christians are told to do.

"You have heard that it was said, 'You shall love your neighbor and hate your enemy. But I say to you, love your enemies, bless those who curse you, do good to those who hate you, and pray for those who spitefully use you and persecute you." (Matthew 5:43-44) What believer would not admit hating your enemy comes easier than loving him?

"Pray without ceasing." (1 Thessalonians 5:17) Although it is an area where we desire to excel, what Christian (if he is honest) would not admit that at times he struggles with his prayer life?

"But you shall receive power when the Holy Spirit has come upon you; and you shall be witnesses to Me in Jerusalem, and in all Judea and Samaria, and to the end of the earth." (Acts 1:8) It has been proven that relatively few Christians speak to others about their salvation.

"All Scripture is given by inspiration of God, and is profitable for doctrine, for reproof, for correction, for instruction in righteousness, that the man of God may be complete, thoroughly equipped for every good work." (2 Timothy 3:16) Yet many

Christians admit that they are not nearly as consistent as they would like to be in their study of the Word to find out how they ought to live.

"And let us consider one another in order to stir up love and good works, not forsaking the assembling of ourselves together, as is the manner of some, but exhorting one another, and so much the more as you see the Day approaching." (Hebrews 10:24-25) We all know those believers who are better at provoking us than provoking us unto love and good works! And as verse 25 mentions, some believers neglect involvement in a local church.

It becomes obvious that living the Christian life is not always easy. That is one reason that if our eternal security and the assurance of it were based on our performance, nobody could ever be certain he was going to heaven. God will do His part, but we might not do ours.

The reason living the Christian life is difficult is that it is a supernatural life. *God is not even expecting us to live it.* What He is asking us to do is to let Him live it through us. That is again why Paul said in Galatians 2:20, "I have been crucified with Christ; it is no longer I who live, but Christ lives in me; and the life which I now live in the flesh I live by faith in the Son of God, who loved me and gave Himself for me."

### *The importance of abiding in Christ*

This is where the book of 1 John comes in with its emphasis on abiding. As mentioned earlier, the book of John was written to tell us how to receive eternal life (John 20:31) and mentions the word "believe" 98 times. The epistle of 1 John was written to tell us how to get close to the One we have come to (1 John 1:3) and mentions the word "abide" 24 times. You come to Christ through believing and get close to Him through abiding.

The late Dr. Dwight Pentecost had the best definition of abiding I have ever heard. He explained that a fish abides in the water when it draws from the water all it needs to swim. A bird abides in the air when it draws from the air all it needs to fly. We abide in Christ when we draw from Him all we need to live the Christian life. We recognize that we cannot live the Christian life and we ask Him to live it through us. In other words, it is walking in His strength not in ours.

**We abide in Christ when we draw from Him all we need to live the Christian life.**

How does this help with assurance of our salvation? Because we recognize that 1 John is not written to give us proofs of whether or not we are saved, but to explain to us how that abiding in Christ helps us live a life that otherwise we could not live. It speaks to living the Christian life, not entering the Christian life.

For example, carefully read 1 John 2:3-6. "Now by this we know that we know Him, if we keep His commandments. He who says, 'I know Him,' and does not keep His commandments, is a liar, and the truth is not in him. But whoever keeps His Word, truly the love of God is perfected in him. By this we know that we are in Him. He who says he abides in Him ought himself also to walk just as He walked."

To say that unless one keeps the commandments, she is not a Christian is to miss the point of the verse. It would also mean that one day we are a Christian and another day we are not. What believer, if he is honest, would say that he keeps the commandments every day? The word "know" is *not* the same Greek word for "know" used in 1 John 5:13 that means to know absolutely. Instead, it is the word "know" that means to know by experience — the experience of walking with Him one day at a time. Notice the emphasis, "But whoever keeps His Word, truly the love of God is *perfected* In Him." We have that love perfected in us through abiding. We can know Christ as Savior, but it is through abiding and the experience of walking with Him that we can live for Christ and keep His commandments. If we say we know Him in the sense of walking with Him and do not keep His commandments, we are not speaking the truth. Entering the Christian life and living the Christian life are two different things.

Continue reading. Three verses later we are told, "He who says he is in the light, and hates his brother, is in darkness until now. He who loves his brother abides in the light, and there is no cause for stumbling in him. But he who hates his brother is in darkness and walks in darkness, and does not know where he is going, because the darkness has blinded his eyes." (vv.9-11)

John is not encouraging anyone to doubt his salvation if he does not love his brother. The fact that he is talking about loving a "brother" affirms that he is talking to believers. He is saying that only when we abide in Christ are we able to walk in light instead of darkness, prevent ourselves from stumbling as believers, and are able to love our brother as we should. You do not *enter* the

Christian life by loving your brother, but once you have entered the Christian life you *live* it by loving your brother. If we have become a Christian and are not loving our brother, we are not abiding in Him.

That understanding of 1 John is what gives two verses in the third chapter of 1 John such meaning. Instead of encouraging one to doubt his salvation or seek proof that he is a Christian, it points to the power of abiding. 1 John 3:5-6 reads, "And you know that He was manifested to take away our sins, and in Him there is no sin. Whoever abides in Him does not sin. Whoever sins has neither seen Him nor known Him." Because all believers sin, some to ease their conscience insert the words, "Whoever abides in Him does not *continue in sin*" — words that are not in the original language. How then could one know that he is saved? How long is "continue"? A month? A year? Five years? Ten years? What kind of sin? Is theft okay, but not adultery? Imagine the uncertainty of one's salvation and the confusion when 1 John 5:13 says we are to know absolutely that we are saved.

Instead, all that 1 John 3:5-6 is saying is that sin is *never* the result of an abiding experience. Whenever we sin it is because (whether it be for one second, one minute, one hour, or one day) we were not abiding in Christ. I once heard the late Dr. Dwight Pentecost asked, "If someone abides in Christ 100% of the time, would he ever sin?" He rightly answered, "No!" When we sin it means at that second or moment we have not seen or known Him in the sense of abiding. Once more, he is talking about living the Christian life, not entering it.

The difference between believing in Christ and abiding in Him is clearly seen in John 8:30-32 — one of the few passages in the gospel of John that talks about abiding. "As He spoke these words, many believed in Him. Then Jesus said to those Jews who believed in Him, "If you abide in My Word, you are My disciples indeed. And you shall know the truth, and the truth shall make you free." One thing that marks a disciple (a subject we will discuss next) is the desire to abide in Him and learn more of His life changing truths. Abiding in Christ is what helps one who is a disciple live the life that God wants Him to live.

## Conclusion

The accurate handling of Scripture means that whatever passage we read, we must ask, "Is this talking about entering the Christian life or living it?" The Scriptures do not confuse the two and we ought not either. To confuse the two is to not only make one of the greatest mistakes in handling Scripture but it can also cause one to either misunderstand the simplicity of salvation or erode the assurance of it.

• • •

## QUESTIONS FOR REFLECTION

1.  How in one sentence is entering the Christian life easy whereas living it can be difficult?

2.  In what ways in the New Testament were believers cautioned not to fall back into the behavior that characterized them as unbelievers?

3.  How in one sentence would you define "abiding in Christ"?

4.  When you think of areas you could fail in your Christian walk, how does "abiding in Christ" help you?

# CHAPTER TWELVE

## *Salvation versus discipleship*

Just as many confuse entering the Christian life with living the Christian life, they also confuse salvation and discipleship. In so doing, some misunderstand the terms of salvation, others fail to move beyond their initial conversion, and still others become confused and lack assurance that they actually know the Lord.

*Eternal life is free.*

As has been repeatedly emphasized, eternal life is a free gift.

As Christ spoke to the Samaritan woman of John 4, He told her, "If you knew the gift of God, and who it is that says to you, 'Give Me a drink,' you would have asked Him, and He would have given you living water." (v.10) Romans 6:23 so plainly says, "For the wages of sin is death, but the gift of God is eternal life in Christ Jesus our Lord." The last chapter of the book of Revelation contains those exciting words, "And the Spirit and the bride say, 'Come!' And let him who hears say, 'Come!' And let Him who thirsts come. Whoever desires, let him take of the water of life freely." (Revelation 22:17)

Eternal life is free to us because Christ paid the price. That Good News is defined in 1 Corinthians

**Eternal life is free to us because Christ paid the price.**

15:3-5 as Christ died for our sins and rose from the dead. Since the price of our sins was paid for through His death and resurrection, God can now extend eternal life as a free gift to all who will receive it. Whosoever will may come! And to those who do, Christ promised, "I am the resurrection and the life. He who believes in Me, though he may die, he shall live. And whoever lives and believes in Me shall never die." (John 11:25-26)

*Discipleship involves a cost.*

A disciple is a learner. The Greek word *mathetes* means learner, one who follows the teachings of another. Hence, a disciple in the New Testament is someone who, having come to Christ, wants to follow after Him and learn more about Him. How do we know that being a Christian and being a disciple are two different things?

> **Hence, a disciple in the New Testament is someone who, having come to Christ, wants to follow after Him and learn more about Him.**

The answer can be reduced to one sentence. *Throughout the New Testament whereas salvation is free, discipleship involves a cost.* So much so, that Christ became concerned about those who got excited about the idea and did not first consider the cost. Prior to defining discipleship, we are told in Luke 14:25, "Now great multitudes went with Him. And He turned and said to them..." "Turned" has the idea of turning abruptly. It is as though He was saying, "Now wait a minute. Hold on! Don't get too excited! Let me explain something. Before you commit to being my disciple, first consider the cost." He then explained the cost of being a disciple.

*What are those costs?*

"If anyone comes to Me and does not hate his father and mother, wife and children, brothers and sisters, yes, and his own life also, he cannot be My disciple. And whoever does not bear his cross and come after Me cannot be My disciple. And whoever does not bear his cross and come after Me cannot be My disciple." (Luke 14: 26-27)

*Following Christ as a disciple costs in three ways.*

First, loyalty to Christ has to have priority over any other earthly ties. Note how specific and descriptive Christ is. "If anyone comes to Me and does not hate his *father* and *mother*, *wife* and *children*, *brothers* and *sisters*, yes, and his own life also, he cannot be My disciple." By "hate" He is not meaning to actually hate those of our family. He is making a comparison. His point is that our loyalty to Christ has to be so strong that all other loyalties and allegiances seem like hate in comparison. Loyalty to Him has to have priority over any other earthly ties. There must be no one who solicits as much devotion from you as He does. He is first in your life; all others are second.

Second, Jesus Christ must have the ownership of your life. Notice He adds, "and his own life also." That means that instead of you deciding what you want to do with your life, He decides. You must be willing to sign your name at the bottom of a sheet of paper and let Him fill it in. You are the directed, He is the director. You relinquish control of your life and place it in His hands to do with it as He pleases. It is an attitude of heart that does not say, "May *my* will be done" but "May *thy* will be done." That is why one must come to Christ recognizing He is the Lord God Almighty, but making Him "Lord" in terms of letting Him control our lives is part of discipleship and spiritual growth not salvation. There are even areas of our lives that we do not recognize that we are giving Him control until we follow Him, and learn more about Him.

The third cost may be the greatest of all. You must be willing to suffer humiliation, hardship, and even death for His sake. His words were, "And whoever does not bear his cross and come after Me cannot be My disciple." The terms "bear his cross" needed no explanation to His listeners. It was the place where they crucified anyone who opposed the will of Rome and those they considered the worst of criminals — a place of humiliation and death. His point was that you need to be willing to accept any persecution you receive and you are fully aware that you may be called upon to suffer death for His sake, as many have.

We can immediately see the difference between becoming a Christian and being a growing disciple. One can be a secret Christian in the sense that he could sincerely trust Christ in the privacy of his home and be hesitant to tell someone. As mentioned earlier, you have an example of that in John 12:42. "Nevertheless even among the rulers many believed in Him, but because of the Pharisees they did not confess Him, lest they should be put out of the synagogue." But it is difficult to desire to be a disciple and maintain a secrecy about it. The secrecy will impact the discipleship, or the discipleship will impact the secrecy.

**The secrecy will impact the discipleship, or the discipleship will impact the secrecy.**

It is also possible to commit to being a disciple one day, month, or year, and draw back on the commitment for any number of reasons at a future time. An example of that is Demas whom Paul mentions in 2 Timothy 4:10. "For Demas has forsaken me, having loved this present world, and has departed for Thessalonica — Crescens for Galatia, Titus for Dalmatia." Demas was a trusted fellow-laborer with Paul as seen in Colossians 4:14 and Philemon 24. Apparently, he was so excited about being a disciple that he wanted to live with Paul and die with him. But when he came to Rome and saw the contrast between the prison that Paul and Epaphras endured and the outer world, everything changed. He saw the gorgeous homes of the rich and the glamor society offered. That became a lot more appealing to him than to follow the path of being a growing disciple.

That is where Matthew 10:27-33 becomes so meaningful. "Whatever I tell you in the dark, speak in the light; and what you hear in the ear, preach on the housetops. And do not fear those who kill the body but cannot kill the soul. But rather fear Him who is able to destroy both soul and body in hell. Are not two sparrows sold for a copper coin? And not one of them falls to the ground apart from your Father's will. But the very hairs of your head are all numbered. Do not fear therefore; you are of more value than many sparrows. Therefore whoever confesses Me before men, him I will also confess before My Father who is in heaven. But whoever denies Me before men, him I will also deny before My Father who is in heaven."

Christ is not talking about denying that one is a believer. The context is discipleship. Three verses earlier He told them,

"A disciple is not above his teacher, nor a servant above his master." (v.24) He is talking about denying that one has been a faithful disciple. That is the same idea expressed in Luke 9:26. "For whoever is ashamed of Me and My words, of him the Son of Man will be ashamed when He comes in His own glory, and in His Father's, and of the holy angels." The context is clearly discipleship. Three verses earlier you have the same thought as expressed in Luke 14:26-27. Luke 9:23 reads, "Then He said to them all, "If anyone desires to come after Me, let him deny himself, and take up his cross daily, and follow Me."

So many turn the beautiful message of the gospel backwards. We are not saved through our surrender to God but through Christ's surrender to the Father. (John 10:18) We are saved when as sinners, we recognize Christ died for us and rose again, and trust in Christ alone to save us. (John 6: 47) The surrender of our lives to Him for however He wants to use us is then part of discipleship and growth.

Receiving eternal life is a once for all decision whereby one appropriates by faith what Christ did on his behalf. And even if that person (after becoming a believer) should turn his back on God, God will not turn His back on him. "For the gifts and calling of God are irrevocable." (Romans 11:29) Growing as a disciple, though, involves daily decisions in which I am willing to bear the costs of being a disciple. Those costs can come in any number of ways — false accusations, humiliation, lack of promotion, friends who avoid us, family members who are upset with our commitment to follow Christ, loss of finances because of priorities that do not surround money, those who exclude us instead of including us at social gatherings, or even martyrdom for the cause of Christ.

That is why as one reads the four gospels, he has to answer the question about particular passages, "Is this talking about becoming a Christian or about becoming a committed disciple?" To not recognize that distinction could cause one to unnecessarily question his salvation or lack the assurance of it. John is the one book written to tell us how to receive eternal life. (John 20:31) Matthew, Mark, and Luke on the other hand, although they contain passages that speak to our eternal salvation, were largely written to talk about discipleship. That is why they speak of living life with a Kingdom mindset, being the salt of the earth and a light and witness to the world, serving God instead of money, forgiving others as God forgave you, being faithful in marriage, faithfulness in handling time, money, and talents, preparing for the second coming of Christ, growing in our faith, our actions and attitudes towards the family of God, endurance as we approach end-time events, prayer and obedience, going into all the world with the gospel, and a host of other subjects — all of which relate to being a learner and a committed follower of Christ.

**That is why as one reads the four gospels, he has to answer the question about particular passages, "Is this talking about becoming a Christian or about becoming a committed disciple?"**

The same is true of other New Testament passages. The issue being addressed is not coming to Christ but following after Him and being obedient to Him as a disciple. We must always ask, "Is this passage speaking to how to come to Christ?" or "Is this passage speaking to how to follow after Christ as His growing disciple?"

We ought to ask, "What is the first thing Christ taught His disciples?" Whatever was first with Him ought to be first with us. Matthew 4:18-19 contains the answer — evangelism. "And Jesus, walking by the Sea of Galilee, saw two brothers, Simon called Peter, and Andrew his brother, casting a net into the sea; for they were fisherman. Then He said to them, 'Follow Me, and I will make you fishers of men.'" He wanted to take them from being fishers of fish to fishers of men.

To use that passage to say that unless one evangelizes they are not a Christian is to mishandle Scripture. Nowhere does the Bible say that. Christ is speaking to those whom He has called as disciples and who accepted such an invitation. One might be a Christian and not talk to another person about his need of the Savior. Sadly, many Christians don't. But one cannot be a *disciple* without in some way being involved in reaching others for Christ. Evangelism is an issue of discipleship, not salvation.

### The differentiations

With the above in mind, note the following distinctions between being a Christian and being a growing disciple:

Eternal life is free; discipleship involves a cost.

In inviting people to eternal life, Christ in essence says, "Whoever will may come." In inviting people to be a disciple, Christ in essence says, "Stop and consider the cost."

Receiving eternal life is unconditional; any sinner anywhere can be saved. Discipleship is conditional, only available to those who are willing to bear the costs.

Receiving eternal life is a once for all decision of trusting Christ as Savior; discipleship involves daily decisions in following after Him.

The gift of eternal life can never be revoked. Even if we turn our back on Christ, He does not turn His back on us. A decision to follow Christ can be revoked.

Eternal life focuses on the matter of salvation; discipleship focuses on the matter of surrender.

Eternal life focuses on what Christ has done for you in the past; discipleship focuses on what you can do for Him in the present and the future.

### *The Bottom Line*

The bottom line is that all Christians ought to be committed disciples; but not all Christians are committed disciples. The reason is that whereas eternal life is free; growing discipleship involves costs which must be considered before making such a commitment. To confuse the two is to confuse the message behind the gospel with the message behind discipleship.

**The bottom line is that all Christians ought to be committed disciples; but not all Christians are committed disciples.**

One can come to Christ and not surrender his life to Him. That is a tremendous mistake because nobody knows better how to make our lives count than Christ does. At the same time, God never extended His free gift on the basis of what that person would then do for God, but on the basis of what God has already done for him. That is one reason it is called the gospel of grace — favor we do not deserve.

## Conclusion

Eternal life could not be any freer. Discipleship, at times, could not be any costlier. Eternal life can only be received if one is willing to accept it as what God calls it — a free gift. Discipleship cannot be entered into unless one first considers the costs.

● ● ●

## QUESTIONS FOR REFLECTION

1. How in one sentence would you explain the difference between salvation and discipleship?

2. How is understanding the difference between being a Christian and becoming a disciple essential to assurance of one's salvation?

3. What are ways that being a disciple could cost you personally?

# CONCLUDING THOUGHTS

# CHAPTER THIRTEEN

## If salvation is guaranteed, why "sell out" for Christ?

A simple truth taught throughout Scripture is that it could not matter less what we were doing before we were saved. God saves sinners anyone, anywhere. Paul's testimony was proof of that. In essence he said, "God saved me to prove He can save anybody." He wrote, "This is a faithful saying and worthy of all acceptance, that Christ Jesus came into the world to save sinners, of whom I am chief. However, for this reason I obtained mercy, that in me first Jesus Christ might show all long-suffering, as a pattern to those who are going to believe on Him for everlasting life." (1 Timothy 1:15-16)

The Bible clearly teaches that although it could matter less what we were doing before we were saved. But the Bible also teaches that it could not matter more what we have been doing since we were saved. Paul said to Titus, "This is a faithful saying, and these things I want you

**But the Bible also teaches that it could not matter more what we have been doing since we were saved.**

to affirm constantly, that those who have believed in God should be careful to maintain good works. These things are good and profitable to men." (Titus 3:8)

Why does it matter what we have been doing since then? If our salvation is guaranteed, what difference does it make how we live? We are going to heaven, right? To express it another way, if our salvation is guaranteed, why "sell out" for Christ? How are good works "good and profitable to men?"

Nowhere in the Scripture is the idea taught, "Because if you don't, then you are really not saved" — something that would take away any assurance of eternal life. Some days we may do well and other days we may perform poorly as believers. As has been stressed repeatedly we are saved on the basis of what He has already done for us, not what we promise to do for Him.

*There are multiple reasons.*

One reason we ought to live for Him is the sheer fact that He died for us. 2 Corinthians 5:15 tells us, "And that He died for all, that those who live should live no longer for themselves, but for Him who died for them and rose again." What better response can we give to the cross than "Here is my life; I will live it for you"?

Another reason is that just as He is holy, holiness ought to be our goal as well. 1 Peter 1:15-16 tells us, "But as He who called you is holy, you also be holy in all your conduct, because it is written, "Be holy, for I am holy." Paul admonished his readers in the same way when he said, "...For just as you presented your members as slaves of uncleanness, and of lawlessness leading to more lawlessness, so now present your members as slaves of righteousness for holiness." (Romans 6:19) Our character ought to reflect His.

A life lived for Him is our way of saying "thank you." What better way is there to reflect an "attitude of gratitude" for what He has done for us? Romans 12:1 expresses it well. "I beseech you therefore, brethren, by the mercies of God, that you present your bodies a living sacrifice, holy, acceptable to God, which is your reasonable service."

A life lived for Him should also reflect our confidence that He could return at any minute. In other words, we do not simply look back at the cross, but we look forward to His return. We take seriously the words of 1 John 2:28. "And now, little children, abide in Him, that when He appears, we may have confidence and not be ashamed before Him at His coming."

No small factor has to be the way that we glorify God before men. Christ admonishes us in Matthew 5:16, "Let your light so shine before men, that they may see your good works and glorify your Father in heaven."

*But there is another reason.*

The Scriptures give another reason for "selling out" for Christ. One that, although prominent in Scripture, is not spoken enough about in our churches. It is the biblical teaching on rewards.

The last chapter of the Bible says, "And behold, I am coming quickly, and My reward is with Me, to give to every one according to his work." (Revelation 22:12) A proper understanding of salvation versus rewards shows the love and fairness of God. He is loving in that whosoever will may come. But He is also fair in that those who live for Him are abundantly rewarded.

Simply put, all saved people get to heaven. All saved people are not equally rewarded. Paul alluded to that in a passage mentioned earlier when he said, "Do you not know that those who run in a race all run, but one receives the prize? Run in such a way that you may obtain it. And everyone who competes for the prize is temperate in all things. Now they do it to obtain a perishable crown, but we an imperishable crown." (1 Corinthians 9:24-25) That is another reason that although it does not matter what you were doing before you were saved, it could not matter more what you have been doing since then. Paul even warned the people in Colossae about the danger of being cheated out of their reward by those who wished to lead them into false doctrine. (Colossians 2:18)

> **Simply put, all saved people get to heaven. All saved people are not equally rewarded.**

That is what makes our time on earth so critical. We have but one chance to earn those rewards. *This is not a trial run; this is it.* When Christ returns, it will be a day of rejoicing for those who have trusted Him and lived for Him. For those who have not lived for Him, they will be thrilled to see the Savior face to face as those who have been saved by His grace. But they will wish more than ever that they would have lived their lives for Him. A time is coming when it will be too late to change. That is why Revelation 22:10 says, "for the time is at hand" and follows that with, "He who is unjust, let him be unjust still; he who is filthy, let him be filthy still; he who is righteous, let him be righteous still; he who is holy, let him be holy still." Ignoring the warnings of Scripture will have permanent consequences. There is no "second life" to live.

When we look into His face we will all wish we would have done even more for the Savior. There will be those believers though that when they stand before the Lord although saved by grace and forever His, will regret that they did not lives for Him. And now, they have no chance to live their lives again. A believer who stands before the Lord having not lived for Him wins and loses. He wins in the sense that he is forever in heaven, thanks to the grace of God. He loses in the sense that he will see what his life could have counted for and didn't and has no chance to live it again. He will be grateful that he is with the Lord but regretful that he was not more serious about Kingdom living.

**A believer who stands before the Lord having not lived for Him wins and loses.**

There will be others that will be delighted that they made their lives count as they are abundantly rewarded.

There are some believers who say, "I do not care of I don't get rewarded. Being in heaven will be enough." Such a person has not taken a serious look at 2 Corinthians 5:9-11. "Therefore we make it our aim, whether present or absent, to be well pleasing to Him. For we must all appear before the judgment seat of Christ, that each one may receive the things done in the body, according to what he has done, whether good or bad. Knowing, therefore, the terror of the Lord, we persuade men; but we are well known to God, and I also trust are well known in your consciences."

That is an easy thing to say now but wait until that person actually looks into the loving eyes of the One who died for him. How we have lived will matter more than it has ever mattered before. The "terror of the Lord" is not a reference to hell. Instead, it refers to standing before a holy, awesome, and all-knowing God having all we have done exposed and evaluated. For the apostle Paul, this was a powerful motive for having a sincere and effective ministry. He wanted to please Him not just because he would be with Him (v.8), but knowing that He, the one who died for Him, would be evaluating his work.

*Is the possibility of being rewarded a proper motive?*

Some believers question, "Is it a proper motive to want to be rewarded?" The answer is most definitely when it is done in the right spirit. That is, we recognize that we are undeserving of anything good that comes from His Hand. At the same time, we want to so live for Him that when we see Him face to face, we hear Him say, "Well done, good and faithful servant." (Matthew 25:23) How better could we honor the One who died for us?

Imagine yourself sent on a particular assignment by a supervisor you greatly respected, admired, and loved. Upon completing that assignment, what would mean more coming from a person of his stature in your life than to hear him say, "Well done, good and faithful servant"? It is the anticipation that Paul must have felt as he came to the end of his life and said, "I have fought the good fight, I have finished the race, I have kept the faith. Finally, there is laid up for me the crown of righteousness, which the Lord, the righteous Judge, will give to me on that Day; and not to me only but also to all who have loved His appearing." (2 Timothy 4:7-8)

*Rewards are strongly addressed in Scripture.*

There are times in Scripture that eternal life itself is seen as a reward, although it cannot be earned. God will be pleased that we are with Him forever. "So Jesus answered and said, "Assuredly, I say to you, there is no one who has left house or brothers or sisters or father or mother or wife or children or lands, for My sake and the gospel's who shall not receive a hundredfold now in this time — houses and brothers and sisters and mothers and children and lands, with persecution — and in the age to come eternal life." (Mark 10:29-30) What better reward for one who has experienced persecution than to spend eternity based on His trust in Christ as Savior in the presence of God forever?

That is one reason the Bible also mentions the concept of "crowns" like athletes who receive crowns for winning their competition. Different crowns are referred to such as a crown of rejoicing for leading others to the Savior (I Thessalonians 2:19), a crown of righteousness for those who love His appearing (II Timothy 4:8), and a crown of life for suffering through trials (James 1:12) They speak to the matter of reward.

No paragraph of the Bible is referred to more concerning the biblical teaching of rewards than 1 Corinthians 3:11-15.

"For no other foundation can anyone lay than that which is laid, which is Jesus Christ. Now if anyone builds on this foundation with gold, silver, precious stones, wood, hay, straw, each one's work will become clear; for the Day will declare it, because it will be revealed by fire; and the fire will test each one's work, of what sort it is. If anyone's work which he has built on it endures, he will receive a reward. If anyone's work is burned, he will suffer loss; but he himself will be saved, yet so as through fire."

Some works are worthy of reward, and some are not. Since fire was used in the New Testament to test the quality of metals, it is a most fitting analogy. Gold, silver, and precious stones represent that which is durable and worthy of reward. Wood, hay, and straw represent that which is neither durable nor worthy of reward. The difference may be in what was done or the attitude in which it was done. God will determine what is worthy of reward and what isn't. It must be noted reward is lost, salvation is not. The Scriptures plainly state, "he himself will be saved, yet so as through fire." The examining results in loss of reward not loss of salvation.

**We do not know much about what those rewards will be but they appear to have something to do with reigning with Christ in eternity.**

Not only did John in Revelation speak of reward and Paul in 1 Corinthians, but Peter did as well. To those who endure in the midst of trials he said, "that the genuineness of your faith, being much more precious than gold that perishes, though it be tested with fire, may be found to praise, honor, and glory at the revelation of Jesus Christ." (1 Peter 1:7)

We do not know much about what those rewards will be but they appear to have something to do with reigning with Christ in eternity. Revelation 2:26 tells us, "And he who overcomes, and keeps My works until the end, to him will I give power over the nations." The point is, we will be rewarded. Who better is there to extend those rewards than an all-knowing God of truth and grace?

One might well ask, "But what about a child that dies at an early age, or one killed in an accident early in life and has little or no chance to earn reward?" There we have to fall back on the question Abraham asked in Genesis 18:25, "Will not the judge of all the earth do what is right?" and be assured that He will. We can rest in the fact that all that is in the hands of a loving and sovereign God. He is too loving to do wrong and too wise to make a mistake.

A passage often overlooked that ties three ideas together is 1 Timothy 2:11-13.

"This is a faithful saying; for if we died with Him, we shall also live with Him. If we endure, we shall also reign with Him. If we deny Him, He also will deny us. If we are faithless, He remains faithful; He cannot deny Himself."

The three ideas found there are (1) there is reward for following Christ — "We shall also reign with Him" (2) If we deny Him, He will deny that we have been a faithful disciple — "If we deny Him, He also will deny us" and (3) even if we turn our back on Him, He cannot and will not turn His back on us — "if we are faithless, He remains faithful; He cannot deny Himself." In a few words God captured the idea that we are forever secure in Christ, how we live after we are saved could not matter more, and there is reward for those who "sell out" for Christ.

## *Conclusion*

The entire principle of rewards is why, for all of us, salvation ought to be the starting point, not the stopping point in our lives. Following Peter's admonition to "grow in the grace and knowledge of our Lord and Savior Jesus Christ" (2 Peter 3:18) we should live a sold out life for Christ. In the end there will be abundant reward with no regrets as we enjoy those rewards while we are celebrating life with the King of Kings.

● ● ●

## QUESTIONS FOR REFLECTION

1. How does a Christian personally suffer if he or she sees salvation as the stopping point instead of the starting point?

2. Why is the principle of rewards a proper motive for living for Christ?

3. How should the principle of reward impact activities/things you are doing right now? Be specific.

# GET EQUIPPED & ENCOURAGED

## AT EVANTELL.ORG

### TAKE OUR FREE PERSONAL EVANGELISM ONLINE COURSES

SEE ALL COURSES AT
*EVANTELL.ORG/ONLINE-TRAINING*

### VIEW OUR TOPIC-BASED TRAINING LIBRARY

BROWSE HOURS OF
CONTENT THAT COVER THE
HOTTEST TOPICS AT
*EVANTELL.ORG/VIRTUAL-EVENTS*

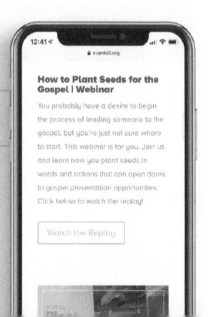

DOWNLOAD OUR APP
FOR EVANGELISM TRAINING
ON-THE-GO

VISIT YOUR APP STORE
AND SEARCH *"EVANTELL"* TO
DOWNLOAD TODAY

VISIT OUR STORE
FOR BOOKS, TRACTS,
AND MORE RESOURCES

VISIT *EVANTELL.ORG/STORE* TO SEE OUR FULL
COLLECTION OF BOOKS AND RESOURCES